THE UNVEILING SECRETS OF A PURPOSEFUL DRIVEN LIFE

EDWIN ENOMHENSIKE I

LifeRich
PUBLISHING®

LifeRich Publishing books may be ordered through booksellers or by contacting:

LifeRich Publishing
1663 Liberty Drive
Bloomington, IN 47403
www.liferichpublishing.com
844-686-9607

ISBN: 978-1-4897-3048-0 (sc)
ISBN: 978-1-4897-3047-3 (hc)
ISBN: 978-1-4897-3049-7 (e)

Library of Congress Control Number: 2020916385

Print information available on the last page.

LifeRich Publishing rev. date: 09/24/2020

DEDICATION

This book is dedicated to the Almighty God. My thoughts and heart also goes to my late dad in the person of Enomhensike Julius Afeyodion.

ACKNOWLEDGEMENT

Foremost, it is important that I express my profound gratitude and also acknowledge my lovely wife- Enomhensike Adeola and my children - Gianna and Giovanni for their immense encouragement and contribution towards the success of the writing, editing and publishing this book. It was indeed a great experience witnessing their undiluted, constructive criticisms and painstaking line by line proof read of this book.

The bible says train a child in the ways of the Lord and he or she will not depart from it. This is an opportunity to acknowledge my parents – Mr. Julius Enomhensike(late) and Mrs. Bridget Enomhensike for their positive direction, nurturing and most importantly the upbringing I got which was in line with the ways of the Lord and a guiding principle in my journey of life on earth.

Special thanks to my author partners and publisher of this book for their professional advice and guidance throughout the process from manuscript stage to the publishing of this great book.

CHAPTER ONE

INTRODUCTION

The mystery of human existence can only be made manifest by the spirit of God. Have you ever contemplated on questions such as where do I come from? What is my purpose on Earth? What is my destiny on earth? And what happens when I die? Most importantly, is God very satisfied with the way I am living on earth?

In order to perfectly understand the process flow of the entire creation and in the light of understanding the purpose of human existence, God sent His only begotten Son to lead and show mankind the way to eternity. Every human being who once and who still exists on this Earth existed to fulfill a particular mission; this is the more reason why you must live by the Word of God and listen to the Holy Spirit to direct and lead your path. In your daily life endeavors and every single decision you take, in order for you to clearly understand why you are on Earth, you honestly need the Holy Spirit. God in His magnificent creation created human life through a process flow, and that is why, for everything you require in life, there is a particular word from the scripture that can perfectly make things work for good in your life through the Holy Spirit; it could be your physical environment, job, profession, marriage, and so on. We as Christians on Earth have a link with God's covenant with Abraham, and working in the atmosphere and understanding of the Abrahamic covenant helps you operate above powers and principalities of this world. You need to understand and apply this covenant at this crucial moment we live in.

One very crucial way you can apply this covenant is by your faith in Christ which you can exercise by your spoken words to any circumstance you are going through. The exercise of your spoken words cannot be overestimated because there is power in your spoken words, and that is why you are wonderfully and fearfully created by our Heavenly Father. You may be going through some precarious times which are sometimes inevitable; if that is prevalent in your life, all you need is to speak the word on that particular situation and it will obey you according to your wish. I know it sounds vague, but I have seen it happen and I have often also applied it to my life.

A long time ago, as a teenager, I was on my way home, and then suddenly the cloud was very heavy. It was as though the cloud wanted to come down. To my greatest astonishment, I was becoming uncomfortable; there were no shelters on the road path and I had several kilometers to cover before I get to my destination. Immediately, a word came to my spirit man, which says, "Son, do you know that you have power over all I have created?" Then I said, "Yes." The word referenced Elijah, Elisha, Moses, and so many men of God as mentioned in the scripture and how they applied faith in His Word. Without any delay and with faith in my inner man, I spoke with a loud voice to the cloud, and believe me, the clouds began to give way. I told her (cloud) not to release the rain until I get to my destination. I applied my Abrahamic covenant through faith in the words I spoke. The cloud obeyed my voice the weather was not sunny and it did not rain. Have you once experienced a pretty weather to an extent that you wouldn't let go? That was the kind of experience I had that lovely day and the best I can ever remember. For hours, I walked to my destination. Immediately I got to my destination, the rain started so heavily with a mighty wind and thunder.

To be honest, that was my first time of applying the covenant I have with God. As a young man, I was uncomfortable with what had happened although I felt pleased in my spirit and began to thank God. I hope you now understand what it means to work and operate with what you have inside of you. If you must know, there are over 366 blessings in the scripture for your life as regards that particular unpalatable situation you are going through. Our Lord Jesus Christ needs those that can trust in Him in all situations of their lives. Before we critically look at the scriptural reasons for human existence, it is pertinent that we read through this short story about a man who once existed on planet Earth.

> *They answered him, we be Abraham's seed, and were never in bondage to any man: how sayest thou, ye shall be made free? John 8:33 KJV*

There lived a young man so many centuries ago who once existed on planet Earth. As he grew up to his tender age, he began to nurse some thoughts. So one day this young man found himself in the midst of people. It was in this gathering he got to discover his biological parents. This was really shocking! So one day, he called his biological parents and asked them just two basic questions, which really gave them the shock of their entire lives. The first question was, "Who am I?" And the second question was, "Why am I on Earth?" The father was short of words. He then said, "ehh…" and in response to the first question, "You are my son," and for the second question, he replied, "you are here to take after me and my possessions when I am gone to the celestial world." Isn't that amazing? As a young man who was highly adventurous and ambitious, he was not satisfied with his father's response. So one day, he took his belongings and left his household in the deep cold winter searching for answers to his questions. As he went further in his journey, having walked all through the day in a remote iced village, he met a group of drunk people. Slowly he reduced his footsteps and approached them, and then asked, "can someone please tell me where I am from and who am I?" One of the men replied, "you are a fool from the forest, hahaha," with a loud voice laughing; they were drunk from strong wine. Another replied, "you are a born miscreant from the zoo, ha ha ha ha." The young man was so heartbroken and knowing fully well that they were drunk and not in the right state to answer his questions, he replied by saying "thank you and God bless you". Thereafter, he continued on his journey. After walking a few miles away from the sight of those fellow drunk countrymen, there was a shopping mall, and this young adventurous man then decided to go into this mall to seek for answers to his questions. He then decided to visit each of the stores one after the other to discover and get answers as to the source of his existence. He visited each store but no one seemed to provide answers to his questions, and so he decided to leave the city to a neighboring village. On his way to the village, the sunset was approaching which led him to getting a shelter. Luckily for him, he saw a little tent with no one inside, so he decided to rest in the tent for the night. As he was deep asleep, he had a dream. In this dream, he saw multiple living souls, all in white garments. During the course of trying to understand where he was, he approached one person from the crowd of people in white garment and said, "please, who are these people and who are you?" The man in white garment replied, "I am me," and then the boy asked, "where are you from?" Then the man in white garment replied, "I am from me." "then why are you here?" asked the boy. "for a purpose," said the man in white garment. The little boy then asked him, "what purpose?" He replied, "for a purpose best known to me and the entire human creation whom I have chosen." This little boy then asked him to assist him with his question of why he was created and why he was here? The strange man then replied, "go to the mountaintop toward the Southeast, and then climb to the mountain peak, when you get to the peak, look down on the Earth what you see belongs to your Heavenly Father and you are responsible for anything that happens to it. You will be held responsible for what so ever happens to it, and you have been mandated to watch over every living thing on the Earth. It is your responsibility to be a blessing and not a curse to the Earth." As he was listening to the man, he woke up from his sleep and began to ponder over all what he heard and his conversation in the dream. From that day henceforth, he began to see life from another perspective. His life was changed for the better and he became stronger as a custodian to everything in his path. He began to see himself as a blessing and not a curse to those around him, his courage and desire is to help everyone he came in contact with change for the better. An example is our Lord Jesus' story of a man that was robbed and attacked by thieves along the road who needed help. Do you know that some passersby including a priest deliberately refused to render help to this helpless man and that a particular person had compassion and was there for this man who needed his help? You need to start seeing that man, that woman, and that child as an opportunity for you to tap into God's blessings through your assistance in any little way.

On June 8 2015, at about 3:50 pm, an incidence happened in my neighborhood. I am narrating this for a reason in order for you to know the importance of being your brother's keeper as the scripture instructed us. I was on my way back in a vehicle from a welder's workshop where I went to inspect some gates he just concluded for my private home. On getting close to where I was to alight from the vehicle, I saw a gathering of people on a major highway which caused huge traffic. Apparently, it was a fatal accident involving a truck and a commercial motorcycle. When I got to the scene of the accident, I could not believe what I saw on the ground. It was a woman in a pool of blood, a crushed body grasping for breath and still struggling to live if given the opportunity. Immediately, I instructed the driver to park so that I will be able to have a clearer picture of what had happened and to also confirm if the woman involved in the fatal accident is someone I know because in the past, a similar accident happened on that same road and I was directly opposite the scene of the accident having a chitchat with neighbours without realizing the victim was a friend's wife. She eventually survived the accident due to our immediate help. As for this woman on the ground who was just involved in an accident, she could not be assisted because her body was decentralized, and nobody wanted to carry her in his or her vehicle without a police escort. Suddenly a young man drove into the scene with his jeep, opened the booth of his car, and pleaded with a policeman to follow him. With the help of others, they were able to lift the woman into the car. I was about to join in carrying the woman, but some good Samaritans quickly carried this woman and put her into the booth of this man's car, and he drove off to the nearest hospital. Everyone around was in shock and anxious. As I was about to leave the scene with a heavy heart, I saw a bank cheque in front of the truck. I also heard people saying she was carrying a baby and the baby had been rushed to a nearby hospital before I got to the scene. Immediately, the Holy Spirit ministered to me that the extent of that crush on her body was a result of that woman trying to protect her child from being killed by the truck.

A few steps away from the scene, I saw a man with sadness written all over his face standing close to his car with his children. Apparently, his wife had gone into that same bank this crushed woman was trying to get into before 4pm. In my country, it is expected that banks should be closed to customers by 4 pm, and this woman was trying to catch up before 4 pm. Reluctantly, she boarded a commercial motorcycle against her wish because they are all over the place with easy access and it is sometimes difficult to get commercial vehicle in that area.

This man narrated what transpired between him, his wife, and that same crushed woman about ten minutes ago before the accident occurred, and that made me feel so bad. He stated that his wife had been sick for over a year. There was a transaction between his wife and a company that mandated her to come to pick up her bank cheque from the company on that same day. On getting to the company, there was a queue, and his wife was directly in front of the woman involved in the accident. When his wife collected her cheque, the woman involved in the accident pleaded with him to wait for ten minutes in order for her to join his family in their vehicle to the bank because he told the woman during a short conversation that his wife will go to the bank from the company which she (the woman) intended going as well, but with the constraint of time, she might not be able to get a vehicle to the bank before the bank close for the day. According to him, the only way she can get to the bank before closing time was to board a motorcycle which was contrary to her wish.

According to this man, she pleaded with him to wait for her so she and her baby could ride with them, but the man bluntly refused to wait for her. So he left with his family in the vehicle. It was not up to ten minutes when the man said he heard people screaming and shouting and saw them gathering adjacent to the Bank where he had parked outside. According to him, his wife just entered the banking hall few minutes before the shouting and cries of people around. On getting to the scene of the accident, he saw that same woman he refused to help just ten minutes ago. This man said he could not believe his eyes and could not tell people what had transpired between him and the woman about ten minutes ago. At this time, his wife was not aware of what had happened because she was in the banking hall trying to clear her bank cheque. Immediately, I left with a grieving heart. On my way home, the Holy Spirit ministered to me saying, "Son, that man was primarily sent to that woman to be her saving grace from a spirit of death around her. If she had survived that day, something would have happened in the spirit realm to the glory of God, but this man refused to help her." The Holy Spirit said that she had a purpose which was about to kick off and the adversary knew, and that was why the enemy of the kingdom gave the man a reprobate heart not to help that woman. I could see the guilt all over the man as the primary cause of what had happened. Trust human being, not human nature.

I remember a film I watched as a little boy; this film was about some aliens from another planet who came into planet Earth just to fulfill a particular mission. One thing that interested me most was that there were always predators and good aliens with distinct mission. These predators or aliens were always programmed in such a way to achieve a particular purpose, and they were committed and dedicated to achieving this purpose and mission for arriving on planet Earth. One very fascinating event was that some of these objectives depending on the mission could be positive or negative. But if negative, there was always a comforter or someone somewhere who will always act as a protective device to prevent the prey from being armed or devoured by the predator. This also applies to us humans; we are all here on Earth on a mission and our existence on Earth is not by mistake or accident. Please get it straight, there is a particular reason why you are here on Earth; the sooner you dig deep and discover this, the better for you as a living soul on Earth.

CHAPTER TWO

WHY ARE YOU ON EARTH?

We humans on earth originated from God and we are a descendant of Abraham. I do not consent to some fallacious or allegory information by a group of people of human origin and their claims that human evolution is from Ape. So many people in our present-day generation live without God's direction and have deliberately refuse to connect with their source of existence. It would interest you to also know that so many people do not know why they are here on planet Earth. We all have a mission to accomplish on Earth, and not until we achieve our mission as human beings, we cannot be fulfilled in our entire physical life and the world beyond. It would interest you to also know that it is apparent to say that so many people live without knowing God's plan for their lives. God has made me understand that most people are contented with their daily routine activities of going to work in the morning, coming back late in the evening, jumping on the TV set, having great weekends, and spending time on some activities that are unproductive to the glory of God. These activities could sometimes be listening to circular music and always engaging in the use of phones which could result to phubbing that has been detrimental to marriages and relationships in our societies and having no quiet time to communicate with their creator and no time to plan for their future and the future of their children. These set of people are satisfied with the little salary they bring back home at the end of every month without knowing how to plan for their future which could be investing and multiplying that little salary they bring back home at the end of the month. It is not a bad idea to plan for the unknown future and commit the unknown future to the known God who has already taken care of the unknown future for a better tomorrow. God has a plan for you, and it depends on you to absolutely and willfully listen to Him and hearken to His voice for a better tomorrow.

> *I must work the works of him that sent me, while it is day: the night cometh, when no man can work. John 9:4 KJV*

Do you know that things do not just happen by accident or for the sake of it happening? For everything that happens to you in life, there is a pre-planned programming for that situation. It amazes me when I hear people say that they are discouraged with life circumstances without knowing that they have power over life as pronounced by God in the process of human creation. Most times when I see some well-matured and grown men in their late fifties, I always wonder how they had lived their youthful life. Most times, when I see such people, I see youthful lost years with no vision and aspiration for a fulfilled life on planet Earth. I have seen people lived a life of night all their lives, and as you rightly know, in the night no man can work effectively which ultimately leads to a life full of penury. So many people had lived a life filled with merriment and forget to plan for their future. I remember when I was still very young, while I was in the high school, I used to have some group of friends who used to laugh at me just because of the fact that I was saving all the money my parents and loved ones gave to me purposely to enroll for my external examinations not because my parents did not have money to give me for my exams but because I had always learnt to live an independent life. I had always wanted to be independent, and before I could get my independence, I needed to convince my parents that I was ready for that. I had always wanted to be out of the umbrella of my parents because I used to see them as being very strict disciplinarians, most especially my dad (may his soul rest in peace). So I made conscious efforts to do everything humanly possible to get out of the house. One day I began to map out strategies; one genuine strategy was for me to make sure I passed my external exam with excellent grades in order for me to gain admission into the university. Being a university student, it is assumed that you are no longer a child and it is presumed that you should be able to take decisions on your own. It is also expected that you should be able to differentiate between what is good and bad. All these translated into my relentless savings for my exams. As accurately planned together with my dedication and focus, I passed my exam excellently and gained admission that same year to one of the best universities in my country. In less than two months after graduating from high school, I was on my way to start receiving lectures in the university. Do you know that this dream came true because I was prepared and planned for it? You will notice that I had reasons for all my actions and was ready to face the consequences, but the primary reason was because I wanted to be out of the umbrella of my parents and be independent. You have to know that life has a precept and this precept is very important to your life and all you do. The word purpose can also be interpreted as a predestined plan and a life that is processed through the breath of God in you when we were created. Now, it is obvious that God has a plan for all his creations, but most people do not know what God's plan and thoughts toward them are and how to achieve this plan concerning their lives. He says,

> *My thought towards you is not of evil but of good, to give you expected end. Jeremiah 29:11 KJV*

Can you see that there is an expected end for you? An expected end means an ending point in one's destination in life that is known. So many people have unconsciously distorted God's plan for their lives.

Your destiny lies in your hand; you have power over everything or circumstances you are currently going through. Come to look at it, when your biological parents gave birth to you, God gave you the ability to take decisions by your sense of reasoning, and that process of reasoning will guide your decision-making in life. I noticed something about a few people I have met in life; these people live and walk in the counsel of the ungodly and sins of this world which is one way of living far away from God's presence. Such lives simply mean that God is not the God of such life which of course leads to a life full of mockery, failure, sickness, anxiety, and so on which is not a good sign of a good living.

> *The thief cometh not, but for to steal, and to kill, and destroy; I am come that they might have life, and that they might have it more abundantly. John 10:10 KJV*

The scripture says that the devil has come to steal your purpose on Earth if you are not in Christ Jesus, and don't forget also that he would not rest until he kills your dream and vision. Spiritually, a man without vision is worse than a blind man, so many people are blind spiritually because the devil has succeeded in killing their visions and aspirations in life. When this happens, victory is of the devil over such life, which means that the devil would have succeeded in destroying such a person's future. But don't you forget what He said in that same verse, which says, "I am come that they might have life (not ordinary life but distinct, superior not inferior, purposeful life) and have it more abundantly" (John 10:10 KJV).

God has a purpose for creating every living creature on Earth. You came into this world one day as a single soul by a process flow that lasted for a period of nine months. Little do I wonder when God said in the scripture that while we were yet in the belly, He knew us (Jeremiah 1:5) and His plan is for everyone to achieve the purpose for which he or she was created. Life itself is based on choice; the decisions we make one way or the other affects our lives and the quality of things we possess, and also the decisions you take today affects your tomorrow. Some people have decided to choose destructive lives, while others have taken wise and prudent decisions that affected not only their lives but those that are within their immediate environment. The ball is in your court; you have a chance to live a life that is worth living and achieve the purpose for which you were created because you have the potential, ability, strength, and capability to achieve your God-given assignment on Earth.

Imagine a ship with a crew without a compass, bearing, and other technology necessary to navigate their way in the deep sea; what do you think would be the result of such a journey as compared to a ship with all crew members with a compass, bearing, and other necessary technology needed for their journey? This is an exemplary analysis of how so many people choose to live on Earth.

> *The Bible said that you are the salt of the Earth and you have savor which helps to make the world a place to live and also you are the light of this world and a city set on a hill that cannot be hidden (Mathew 5:13– 16 KJV).*

I want to thank God for the opportunity of making us part of the chosen ones as salt and light of this world because He has entrusted all the elements in this world to us to manage efficaciously and efficiently. But the question is, are you prudent in your ways of life? Are you efficient in the utilization of this God-given gift to bring out the best in you? Are you living an upright life worthy in the sight of God? All these questions are very important, for the Bible went further in verse 15 and 16 of that same scripture to say that "Neither do men light a candle, and put it under a bushel, but on a candle stick; and it giveth light unto all that are in the house. Let your light so shine before men, that they may see your good works, and glorify your father which is in heaven."

So many Christians have decided to put off their light and also lost the savor of salt that has been bestowed on them, and some have also succeeded in putting off their light and maintaining the savor of the salt, while to others it is the reverse, that is, the light is on, but it is under a bushel and has lost the savor, while the last set of Christians are still keeping up the good work and purpose of God in their lives. These set of Christians as mentioned have succeeded in adding savor to the Earth and made the light so shine that darkness cannot comprehend it.

We have different types of Christians. There are some people that proclaim to be Christians, but their ways of living are entirely different from living an exemplary life of a Christian. These set of people do not bring happiness, love, and blessings to people around them and they have succeeded in bringing down so many lives which has inevitably led to losing the brightness of their lives, while others have lost the brightness of their lives and the good works that are not glorifying to God but maintain the savor in their own ways. These type of Christians do not affect the lives of those around them even with the savor they have. The other type are those that have the light but is not shining forth to affect those around them and has lost their savor on Earth. The last set of Christians are those that have added salt to the world with the savor (the word of God), and their light has so shine to the extent that it has brought down the glory of God in the life of men so that the son of man may be glorified in the heavens and on Earth.

I admonish you to check your life now and know the party you belong, and if you are not in the last category of Christians, you have the opportunity to become the salt and light of this world. I pray that the Lord will open the eyes of your understanding and wisdom for you to realize the evil and danger of not serving God the way you should.

> *I can do all things through Christ Jesus that strengtheneth me. Philippians 4:13 KJV*

You can become who God wants you to be; you can be a tool for the purpose of the kingdom of God on Earth. You can do all things by the power and strength which is the Holy Ghost inside of you. You are the temple of the Holy Ghost. You have the strength and power to become a good Christian by the power of the Holy Ghost. The Holy Spirit can work with you and also direct and give you vision to move forward. Matthew 6:8 KJV says, "be not ye therefore like unto them: for your father knoweth what things ye have need of before ye ask him." The scripture further went:

> *But my God shall supply all your needs according to his riches in glory by Christ Jesus. The Epistle of Paul to the Philippians 4:19 KJV*

Our God is so great and wonderful because He knows what you need to live a good life as a Christian and to also achieve the purpose for which He has created you on planet Earth. There are some times that we need to exercise our rights as Christians and apply them to our daily living. So many Christians are so much satisfied with their present state of circumstances while the devil is busy trading on their soul and has succeeded in taking what has been given to them by God (birthright). Please, for the sake of the account you owe God, you need to understand what you are made of (power), and this also has to be exercised.

> *From the days of John the Baptist until now the kingdom of heaven suffereth violence and the violent take it by force. Mathew 11:12 KJV*

I admonish you today to know that you have to be violent against every negative thing happening in your life that is not pleasing to God. It might be some of that habit, behavior, and attitude of yours that you know fully well do not please God. It might also be the level you are currently operating spiritually, physically, morally, or financially. It is the wish of God that you are comfortable in all you do so that all the praises and glory are ascribed unto Him in Heaven.

Do you know that there are some plants in your life that has to be rooted out? These are plants that you might know and possibly you could be ignorant of, and if this is the case in your life, it will hinder you from achieving your purpose on Earth. This does not glorify God because it slows down the pace of growth in your life. This plant can be sin which is a reproach in your life; it sends God away from your life. You need to have a change of that present situation in your life and change your habit of a sinful life in order to please God and the heavenly host. These plants can also be selfishness, greediness, maliciousness, hatred, envy, and so on. These negative chains can be broken in your life, but the responsibility lies on you alone by the help of the Holy Ghost. If only you can ask for a change of life, He is ever ready to accept you anytime, anywhere.

For what is a man profited, if he shall gain the whole world, and lose his own soul? Or what shall a man give in exchange for his soul? Matthew 16:26 KJV

Is there anything you can exchange for that precious soul of yours? There are so many things you have to let go now; you have to cast them out from your life; only you know these best. God has come to save that which is lost. Lay up not for yourself the treasures upon the Earth which are corruptible, but lay up to yourself the treasures of heaven which are not corruptible and cannot be stolen by the devil. The devil would not rest not until he steals your treasures on Earth which will not glorify God but glorify men on Earth.

But seek ye first the kingdom of God, and his righteousness; and all these things shall be added unto you in heaven and earth. Matthew 6:33 KJV

Be wise now, therefore, in your ways of life, and I strongly recommend that you ask God for direction of your life. The Bible said in the book of Proverbs:

A wise man will hear, and will increase learning; and a man of understanding shall attain unto wise counsels; to understand a proverb and the interpretation; the words of the wise and their dark sayings. The fear of the Lord is the beginning of knowledge; but fools despise wisdom and instructions. Proverbs 1:5–7 KJV

Do not lean on what you presently have or your understanding, but always look up to God, the Author and Finisher of your faith, who can only reveal His purpose for you on Earth only if you accept Him as your Lord and personal Savior who died for you on the cross of Calvary. Do not forget to serve the Lord with your heart and fear Him in all you do; also do not despise the Lord and remember to put your trust in God and God alone in all you do. Moreover, always seek the face of the Lord in your life because He is rewarder of those that diligently seek Him.

CHAPTER THREE

WAYS OF UNDERSTANDING GOD'S PURPOSE FOR YOUR LIFE

Every human on Earth has a particular purpose for existence. Our Lord Jesus Christ had a purpose which was to ultimately reconcile men to God through the redemption of our sins (salvation). Come to think of it, if we carry out a critical comparative analysis of the number of years Methuselah and Jesus Christ spent on Earth, we will discover that the number of years an individual lives on Earth does not positively relate to achieving purpose but by the actualization and fulfillment of God's predestined purpose and mission on Earth. This is made manifest by the revelation through the help of the spirit of God. It is not the number of years that you spend on Earth that matters, but your ability to affect lives positively and create an everlasting reference for yourself.

According to forensic scientist, there are no two souls that have the same fingerprint on Earth. Consider a case of criminal investigation once a finger print is collected, a crime can be traced to the perpetrator. This is why you are you, very unique and wonderfully created by God. No one can be exactly 100% like you with the exact cells, body organs and body shape. In a case of identical twins, there might be some resemblance but one of the twins will have a unique feature that cannot be accurately the same with the other which will always make the difference. The only way to have a trace or find the culprit is by the help of forensic analysis of all fingerprints as revealed during the course of investigation. This also applies to working in accordance to the word of God and His precept of His divine purpose for your life. Every single activity of yours either by your heart, in secret places, or in the open has your fingerprints written on it which facilitates God's ability to record all the events in your life. It is wonderful to know that our Heavenly Father is the only Forensic Scientist that cannot make mistake in any investigation both spiritually and physically. But notwithstanding, according to the scriptures, it says:

> *But ye are a chosen generation, a royal priesthood, a holy nation, a peculiar people; that ye should shew forth the praises of Him who hath called you out of darkness into his marvellous light. 1 Peter 2:9 KJV*

Having knowledge of your purpose is paramount to achieving and working in the realm of your purpose. One pertinent characteristic about the importance of knowledge is that it brings understanding, and understanding in reality the purpose for which you were created helps you achieve God's divine purpose for your life. Have you ever asked yourself why exactly you are on Earth? I indulge you to take time to understand and discover this particular mission of yours.

Understanding is a wellspring of life unto him that hath it; but the instruction of fools is folly. Proverbs 16:22 KJV

An understanding of your purpose on Earth brings a distinctive source of life to your spirit man. This is because when you have an understanding of God's word as it relates to your life's situations, you will start to live a life above those circumstances and you will start to walk and operate toward the right direction for which God wants you to operate. Come to think of it, who told you that you cannot get out of that precarious situation? All you need is wisdom which cometh not but by understanding and understanding cometh not, but by the spirit of God. I guess you might be wondering how the spirit of God can be responsible for your understanding of His purpose for your life and the revelation of the reasons why you might not have been operating in the realm you are supposed to be operating.

Jesus Christ said He is going to send the Comforter that would teach you everything and also that same Comforter will order thy speech. All I need to tell you is that you should not bother yourself on what to say or do to get out of that precarious situation. The spirit of God will direct you and tell you what to do and what not to do and say at the appropriate time. John 15:26 tells us who the Holy Ghost is and where the Holy Spirit proceeded from.

Do you know that the reason why most people are still wallowing in confusion is because they fail to recognize that we are operating in the era of the Holy Ghost? Jesus Christ said that He will go and after that the Comforter will come onto the face of the Earth and the Comforter which is to come, you cannot see physically, but He is always there to help you in all you do. He will give you understanding, direct your footsteps, and give you utterances that would proceed out from thee. We are going to critically look at the various ways your purpose in life can be revealed by God:

- The Holy Ghost
- Dreams

HOLY GHOST

So many Christians in our generation have succeeded in undermining the importance and significance of the Holy Spirit in their lives. God, the creator of the heavens and Earth, knows how important it is to release the third person in the heavenly trinity, and that is why when the Son of man was about to depart from the Earth, He said, "I will send the Comforter which will comfort you in every area of your life." Imagine how loving and kind our Creator is toward human race.

> *But ye shall receive power, after that the Holy Ghost is come upon you; and ye shall be witnesses unto me both in Jerusalem, and in all Judea, and in Samaria, and unto the uttermost part of the earth.* Acts 1:8 KJV

One of the ways you can understand God's purpose for your life is by the help of the "Holy Ghost." Not until you start operating in the atmosphere of recognizing and acknowledging the importance of the Holy Ghost, your understanding of the divine purpose for which you were created will not come into manifestation. God has given you the opportunity to operate and rule the world under the influence of the Holy Ghost, and all you have to do is to be determined by an inner conviction of your spirit man that you need Him to take charge of your life and to also have His way in all you do. Tell Him to take control of your life and also direct all you do, and He will, and when this happens, your life can never remain the same again.

The scripture Acts 1:8A (KJV) says, "But ye shall receive power and after that the Holy Ghost is come upon you." This means that there is a consequence of receiving the Holy Ghost which is power. The question is, have you received the power? And has the Holy Ghost come upon you? You can only receive power by the help of God which comes only when He has been recognized in your life as your Lord and personal Savior. Only when this happens then the Holy Ghost would envelop you and also help you in all you do. He will make you a witness unto the uttermost part of the Earth. When you receive the Holy Ghost, you will receive the power to differentiate between the things of the spirit and your mind. The spirit man in you which is of God will tell you when you are doing things contrary to the will of the almighty God. He will tell you when you are going astray, where to go, and how to live a life worth living, and He will give you understanding of life in its totality, and also the power to make wealth will be bestowed unto you which will exceed men's understanding. Working in an atmosphere under the influence of the Holy Spirit will help you work in the right and positive direction toward God's plan and purpose for your life.

> *And you, that were sometime alienated and enemies in your mind by wicked works, yet now hath he reconciled in the body of his flesh through death, to present you holy and unblameable and unreproveable in his sight. Colossians 1:21–22 KJV*

On the cross, your old man was crucified with him which means that you do not operate under the influence of sin for you have been given the power to live above sin. Having destroyed sin on the cross, He has given us the ability not to serve sin henceforth. This now helps us unblameable in His sight, through the help of the Holy Ghost.

It is pertinent we look at the importance of the Holy Spirit or rather look at the various ways the Holy Spirit can help you successfully complete your heavenly race on Earth. There are several ways, but we will be looking at five scriptural references of the importance of the third person in the Holy Trinity to His chosen generation; these are the following:

- Living above sin

> *For sin shall not have dominion over you: for ye are not under the law, but under grace. Romans 6:14 KJV*

One amazing grace we have as Christians is our supernatural ability to live above sin through the help of the Holy Spirit. Do you know that our Lord Jesus once experienced an attempt by the adversary to sin? But by the help of the Holy Spirit, He was able to conquer the devil and lived above sins. He has also given us that same grace by the help of the Comforter not to be devoured by sins because we are not under any law. Your faith which is much more precious than gold will be put to test, but by the special power you possess by the Holy Ghost, your life will be to the glory of God in praises when you appear in His presence in judgment.

I admonish you to count it all joy when you fall into divers' temptations because the trial of your faith is nothing but by patience in glory through our Lord. Patience is a virtue that helps you overcome sins when faced with divers' temptations because it brings perfection in your ability to perfectly understand the ways of your adversaries. But it is important to note that there is none that is perfect nor righteous in the sight of God, but our ability to be patient and desire to overcome sin gives us a place in the blessings and grace of God to live above sin.

One great and unbelievable sin that has taken so many people to hell is their inability to forgive those that have transgressed against them. I need you to know that the moment you take it as a habit not to forgive your friends, neighbors, and those around that have in one way or another offended you, you are putting your eternal life in danger as you are practically heading to hell. But by the grace which we have received in Christ Jesus, we have been given the ability to forgive those that have in one way or the other offended us. Despite the fact that you were born into sin, I want you to know that you have been washed, sanctified, and justified in the name of the Lord by the Spirit of our God through the redemption that is in Christ Jesus. You have to know that you cannot say that you are in the light when you hate your brother, so you need to consciously cultivate the habit of showing love to one another wherever you find yourself.

The Earth belongs to the Lord and all that is therein, but it will marvel you to know that the love of the world is enmity with God. Having received the grace to live above sin, the love of this world has been automatically taken away from you, and you have been given the grace to start loving the things of God in righteousness and working for the kingdom on Earth. You need to know that just as we were born into sin by Adam, came the gift of grace by the Holy Ghost to live above sin.

You have been given the mandate to pray for those that are still living as a servant to sin. They are all around you. Do not chastise them, but bring them closer and speak the Word to their spirit in order for their souls to be redeemed lest thou also be tempted.

Our God is good and upright, so are we living under grace. He is the head and we are the branches. We are one body in Christ by the help of the Holy Spirit, and living as one body will teach and direct us in all we do.

> *Who His own self bare our sins in His own body on the tree that we, being dead to sins, should live unto righteousness: by whose stripes ye were healed. 1 Peter 2:24 KJV*

Even while we were yet sinners and dead in sins, Christ loved us, and that is why He took it upon Himself to bare our sins on the tree in order for us to live unto righteousness. On the tree, there is an automatic transformation of your life in the right direction. Your steps have been ordered in His word and your iniquity has ceased to have dominion over you. You rose with Him and have been set free from the power of death. Your focus now is supposed to be on the things that are above the Earth for your sinful nature is dead and your life has been in our Lord Jesus Christ in eternity. When He comes again for the saint, you will also be risen with Him unto where He has prepared for you; isn't that wonderful?! What a glorious eternal life after death. When you live above sin, you have supernaturally started working not in the counsel of the ungodly because your desires are in the things of the Lord and the laws of God's creation.

A life above sins is a life that has attracted the heavenly connection in all areas. When individuals, governments, and countries are facing economic crisis, you will be operating under divine and celestial economy which is filled with abundance and grace. When you are operating above sins, no evil plans against you will prosper. This is based on divine law of human creation. A life without sin helps illuminate your spirit to an untouchable state in the spirit realm. When you live above sin, it is an express ticket of being classified in the celestial realm as a good man.

When you operate in this realm, everything that proceeds from your heart is good. You will always want to do good through the help of God, and you will become a blessing to everyone around you. At this point of your life, you have the life of Christ in you as you constantly fellowship with Him.

- Taking right decisions

> *Trust in the Lord with all thine heart; and lean not unto thine own understanding. In all thy ways acknowledge Him and He shall direct thy paths. Proverbs 3:5–6 KJV*

Any man that put his trust on himself has paved way for his downfall. Hear this: you cannot do anything successfully without the help of the Holy Spirit. The Holy Spirit who is your companion is always there for you to take the right decision only if you will allow Him to. Any man that puts his trust in the Lord has from the beginning gotten the end result. David put his trust in the Lord and that was why he defeated Goliath, and he acknowledged God through his spoken words before Goliath was defeated. In your daily activities in life, trust in Him in executing that mission. God's understanding cannot be comprehended and His foolishness is wiser than human understanding. He is the only one that can direct your path in the right direction. Nothing happens by accident. Everything that happens to you on Earth, may I tell you, has been predestined, but you can give the Holy Spirit the opportunity to take you to that place at the right time and prevent you from being in that place at the wrong time. You cannot do it on your own, but by the help of the Holy Spirit.

> *I will instruct thee and teach thee in the way which thou shall go; I will guide thee with mine eye. Psalm 32:8 KJV*

Our God is too passionate and His loving-kindness toward you is remarkably unbelievable. Can you see how loving and caring He is toward you? You are His treasure and you mean a lot to Him; that is why He wants you to succeed in all you do by His divine instructions and lessons through His glory. Do you know that your going out and coming in since you arrived on Earth have been carefully guided by the Holy Spirit? Do you think it is by your power or might or ability that the various successful activities you have been involved in were made possible? But it has been by the knowledge you have derived through the teachings of the Holy Spirit unconsciously. Those successful businesses, job interviews, marriage, academic pursuits, and so on have been made possible by the special grace and instruction of God.

When you take a decision, there is always an expected output of such action. A decision is a by-product of thoughts that have been given birth to in your spirit. As a child of God, there is an expected end from our Lord concerning that plan of yours (Jeremiah 29:11). Be rest assured that the peace of the Holy Ghost in your spirit will give you understanding to perfectly apply the knowledge concerning a successful implementation of your vision into reality to the glory of God. Whenever you are faced with a difficult situation on taking a decision in the face of various alternatives, all you need to do is meet with the great Counselor. He will counsel you on the right decision that will give you peace and joy.

You have to be upright in the ways of the Lord in order for your decisions to flourish because the moment you have received direction on the right decisions and you start to see the positive output of your decisions, you do not think it is by your wisdom because when you start thinking that way, the latter end might amaze you. Always endeavor to give reference to God for every situation that comes your way. Do you remember the rich man in the scripture who thought he had achieved all and to him he was quite doing well out of his own personal efforts? That same night the Lord told him in his dream that his soul will be taken. This is an exemplary illustration of man's inability to reference God in our lives.

> *Thou wilt shew me the path of life: in thy presence is fullness of joy; at thy right hand there are pleasures forever more.*
> *Psalm 16:11 KJV*

There are so many people on Earth that have taken eternal wrong decisions, and such souls have already taken a place of their choice in the world beyond, and it is very unfortunate because they have heard the word of the Lord on several occasions and have refused to hearken unto the voice of the servant of God. These people do not believe in the supremacy of our Lord. There are so many Christians that have completely ignored the importance of Holy Spirit in their Christian race. You cannot win the race without the help of the Holy Spirit. This is because He will show you the right path to eternal life in the presence of God. The sooner you take that quick decision in working for God, the better for you. The day is near in the valley of decision (Joel 3:14 KJV). It is up to you to either take that decision which you will eventually realize when it might be too late.

> *I call heaven and earth to record this day against you, that I have set before you life and death, blessings and cursing: therefore choose life, that both thou and thy seed may live. Deuteronomy 30:19 KJV*

According to the above scripture, a record has been made today toward you according to the Holy Spirit as regards an important decision you have to make on eternity. It is either you choose life or death; you will not hold anyone responsible for the eternal outcome of your decisions. There is still an opportunity now as you are reading this book; choose life, I beg of you by the mercy of God.

- Blessing to your generation

> *And we know that all things work together for good to them that love God, to them who are called according to his purpose. Romans 8:28 KJV*

One of the important criteria scripturally for you as a Christian is to be blessed upon the face of the Earth is for you to be upright in all you do. It is also pertinent to say that another important justification for you to tap into God's blessing is the absolute fear of our Heavenly Father and a complete submission to His commandments. When you keep to His words and adhere to His commandments, your seeds shall be blessed upon the face of the Earth. Wealth and riches shall continually be in your house. You are called for a purpose; that is the more reason why you are blessed, and all things on Earth and in Heaven will if necessary obey the laws of creation specifically for your sake in order for God's blessings to be permanent in your household and generations to come.

There is a multiplier effect of your relationship with God to your generations. When you have a blissful relationship with Him, you are directly and indirectly taking care of your generational needs in the presence of God. He will take it as His responsibility to bless your generations. An example is Abraham and his covenant with God. He was a blessing to his descendants. He kept God's commandments and believed in Him which was counted as righteousness in the sight of God. He kept all that was therein and his seeds multiplied to all nations upon the face of Earth. We are blessed because we are his seeds and we obey the voice of the Lord.

Daniel worked with God in good faith in the sight of God. Daniel while in the palace determined in his heart that he will not eat from the king's portion. Also, Moses did the same, and these singular acts gave them favor in the sight of God. When Moses had become of age while in the palace, he had all the pleasures and good things of life, but by faith he refused to be called the son of pharaoh's daughter because he had pleasures in the things of the Lord. He chose to rather suffer affliction with the people of God rather than enjoy the pleasures of sins for a season.

What are those things that you are currently enjoying that will only last for a season? If you hold these things in high esteem, it is better you throw them off the shelf and begin to start enjoying the pleasures of God forever. If you want to be a blessing to your generations, you need the help of the Holy Spirit. What is that thing you want to be remembered for? I admonish you to start making plans for your third and fourth generation through divine connection with the celestial world. Do you know that when you work with God, you are divinely taken care of? This is because there is no single soul that will have power over your life. If God be for you, who can be against you? There is no one. He will bless them that bless you and curse them that curse you.

> *And I will make thy seed to multiply as the stars of heaven, and will give unto thy seed all these countries; and in thy seed shall all the nations of the earth be blessed. And the Lord appeared unto him the same night, and said, I am the God of Abraham thy father: fear not, for I am with thee, and will bless thee, and multiply thy seed for my servant Abraham's sake. Genesis 26:4, 24 KJV*

Words cannot explain the importance of working with God in good faith. My God keeps to His Word. He cannot fail you when He promises. Man can disappoint you, but God cannot. God had a covenant with Abraham unto his generation to come; even after Abraham had departed from the human flesh, God kept His promise unto his son – Isaac and his generations. When there was famine in the land and everyone was facing financial, economic, and social challenges, Isaac through God's covenant with Abraham operated the heavenly economic principle of abundance. The good thing is that God will not leave you nor forsake you until He has perfected that which He has spoken of you. Do you know the reason why you are still alive today? It is simply because that which the Lord has spoken unto your life has not been manifested. You still have the opportunity to start operating in that plane or realm where God wants you to be operating. When you were created, God pronounced blessings upon your life, but it is the manifestation of these blessings that is yet to be revealed. Do not allow anyone tell you that you are not blessed because you are connected to a covenant-keeping God. All you have to do is ask God for the manifestation of His plans which He has spoken about you and it shall come to stay.

I have heard so many say that they want to leave a particular environment because of some perceived activities of the wicked or evil forces. It is quite unfortunate because these people do not have an insight into what God has done for them spiritually. When we look at the book of the first chapter of Exodus, we will observe that despite all the evil plans of pharaoh towards the children of Israel, they waxed stronger and stronger to a point that the new king was uncomfortable with the growth process of the children of Israel in the midst of the Egyptians. So it is your birthright to be blessed in your business, finances, marriage, and in all that you do.

At this moment, you might be saying in your heart, what does the writer mean by all these sayings? Does he know what I am currently passing through? I have not been able to pay my mortgage, I cannot take care of my bills, I am childless, or I have lost all I once had. I have good news for you: it is for your own good because you might not be ready to handle the treasure which God has deposited in you because you do not have an insight of God's plan for your life. If you read through Deuteronomy chapter 8, you will discover that God deliberately made the children of Israel pass through hard times specifically for their own good. Most importantly, take a look into your life. Is it pleasing to God for Him to release that which He has pronounced when you were created? Despite the fact that you are no longer under the law but under the covenant of Christ, it is pertinent to allow God to take control of your life in order for you to start operating in the Abrahamic covenant.

- Living above fear

> *For God hath not given us the spirit of fear; but of power, and of love, and of a sound mind. 2 Timothy 1:7 KJV*

Fear is a state of physical, emotional, and psychological discomfort as a result of a known or unknown precarious situation facing a man. One of the weapons the adversaries used to overcome a Christian is fear. The adversary knows who you are in Christ Jesus, and he perfectly understands how to steal from you. Imagine yourself in the middle of a forest at night walking through the valley of the imagination of evil; you need to be bold like a Lion in such situation through Christ. You might have been diagnosed with an incurable disease, recently lost your job, and so on; all I want you to know is to exercise the word of God to that particular situation.

When God started the creative process of your existence, He knew what awaits you on Earth which is primarily His purpose for sending you for His glory to be made manifest. He equipped your spirit man with all it needs to perfectly carry out its mission on Earth. Why have you decided to operate below your physical and spiritual potential that is in you? You have not been given a spirit of fear, can't you get it? It is in the word of God. Your spirit has three attributes which are power, love, and sound mind. With these attributes, there is no plan of the adversaries that can limit or stop you from operating in the predestined position in your life.

> *Yea, though I walk through the valley of the shadow of death, I will fear no evil: for thou art with me; thy rod and thy staff they comfort me. Psalm 23:4 KJV*

Our God says through the psalmist that He is with you and not I will be with you. Let's take our shadow as an illustration. Can you explain the mystery behind your shadows at night or in a dark place or closet? It is a mystery that can only be explained by God who created the heavens, the Earth, and all that is therein. I want you to know that He is with you ever since you came into existence. If not for God, you would not have been alive today, so why are you afraid? Do not allow the devil steal your happiness because God Himself will not be happy with you. He is with you anywhere you go, and that is why He is called the omnipresent. He is with you when you go out and come in, when you are awake or asleep. He watches over you all times until the right time when He will call you to His bosom. Speak the word and the devil will flee. Don't be deceived; no man has the power to take your life only if God allows it. You need to start applying God's word and His principle to that situation you are facing. The Bible says, "fear not that which can kill the body alone, but fear He that can kill the body and soul."

Our Lord Jesus was tempted, but He kept to His word and made the adversary understand what had been spoken concerning Him. He was not afraid and neither was He moved by all the plans of the devil which He knew. He was crucified on the cross not because He did not have the power to change the process flow of His purpose on Earth, but He knew and allowed the devil's plan to succeed through Judas for the prophesy to come to pass as spoken by the prophets in the past.

> *For I the LORD thy God will hold thy right hand, saying unto thee, fear not; I will help thee. Isaiah 41:13 KJV*

What a wonderful and glorious God we have and serve in the highest. You are a chosen generation, a royal priesthood unto God, so why are you afraid? He says, "I will help you come out of that situation, I will give you that desired dream, and I will hold your right hand and lead you in the right path." Kindly note that when you are afraid of any situation, you are limiting the entrance of God into your life, so stop being afraid and start operating in the realm of the supernatural. If God be for you as always, who can be against you, and if He blesses you, who can take away His blessings from you?

If you read through Exodus 14:13, you will discover that Moses was trying to admonish the children of Israelites not to be afraid. The question is, why were they afraid? They were afraid because they were confronted by the Egyptian army who sought to devour them. But Moses understood the importance of standing on the word of the Lord through the help of the Holy Spirit, believing that they were victorious right from the beginning. He that sent him is I am that I am. He told them that the Egyptians you see today you shall see them no more. What is that thing that portrays itself as the Egyptians in your life? You have to be strong and be of good courage. Fear not neither be afraid of them, for my God will always go before you and be with you. He will not leave, fail, nor forsake you. By the grace of God, from today you shall see those obstacles no more, in Jesus name, amen!

- Always victorious

> *But thanks be to God, which giveth us the victory through our Lord Jesus Christ. 1 Corinthians 15:57 KJV*

As Christians we are constantly faced with battles of life; it is not because these battles cannot be averted before we are confronted with them. Although victory has been recorded in our favor in the spiritual realm, God allows it as a test of our faith and our trust in Him and a test to also know if we will still be obedient to His commandments. When you are faced with battles of life, our God says that the battles are His and not yours. Despite the fact that those with them are more physically compared to those with you in the physical, it will amaze you that your victory has been assured in Christ Jesus who has paid it all on the cross of Calvary. When He made the pronouncement it is finished, it meant all your battles have been won, your diseases have been taken away, and we are no longer under the laws of man; He became poor so you might be rich and your financial needs have been taken care of.

> *For thou hast girded me with strength unto the battle: thou hast subdued under me those that rose up against me. Psalm 18:39 KJV*

Every battle we face as Christians is a manifestation of the extent of the level of grace we possess to withstand such a battle. God will not allow a battle you cannot withstand to come your way. The strength to be victorious and successful in the midst of such battle has been bestowed upon you before it comes your way. All that is required is for you to put your trust in God and look up to Him, the author and finisher of your faith.

Lean not on your own understanding, personality, or strength, but put your trust in God who alone can give you victory in that battle you are faced with. An example is David and Goliath. Scripturally, it will be revealed that both men had confidence in something which propelled each confrontation in the battlefield. David trusted in the Lord of hosts, while Goliath trusted in his sword and spear with a shield. At the end of the battle, David was victorious over Goliath which was a manifestation of the importance of putting your trust in God and not in man if you want to come out victorious (Psalm 146:3).

Several battles have been fought on your behalf both physically and spiritually by the heavenly host. From the day you had your first breath, there have been several contentions in the spiritual and physical for your soul. Your presence and that mission you are carrying were announced through the first cry as a newborn baby. A good example was the birth of Moses. He had a mission on Earth primarily to be that saving grace and channel of redemption to the children of Israel from the land of captivity. Despite all the challenges he had in carrying out his mission, the Lord stood by him and made him victorious over Pharaoh and his magicians. If you want to be victorious in all you do, you have to focus on God and also dedicate your heart to serving Him. Our Lord Jesus has set an exemplary life ahead of us for He is the head and we are the branches. He has given us a precept of how to become successful in the battles in the world we find ourselves. Despite the fact that He is God, He worked closely with God the father and the Holy Spirit to successfully carry out His purpose on Earth.

Have you been in a situation where everything seems to be working contrary to your expectation and it seems the world is against you? Don't worry, the Earth is the Lord and the fullness thereof, the world and they that dwell therein. Always ensure you handover that situation to God and Him alone, for He cannot share His glory with any man. Always see yourself as victor and not a victim for victory is embedded inside of you.

DREAMS

There are three men scripturally whose birth was announced before their conception in the spirit realm due to their spiritual power, strength, and intended purpose on Earth. These announcements were made through a dream before their birth was physically manifested or by physical appearance of an angel to the preconceived/intended parents who were supposed to nurture and groom these souls up until their maturity for their purpose or ministry to kick off.

These men are Samson, John the Baptist, and Jesus Christ of Nazareth. Two of these great men fulfilled their purpose/mission on Earth, while one of these three great men could not fulfill his mission on Earth as planned but was able to work with God and brought down His glory to the children of the Earth shortly before the devil stole his glory. Let's briefly look at these men and how they were able to fulfill God's plan for their lives and what went wrong with that great man in his journey to fulfilling God's plan for his live (Jeremiah 1:5).

Samson, the son of Manoah, from Zorah, from the tribe of the Danites, was referred to as the strongest man on Earth during his time while living with humanity. His birth was specially planned by God primarily to come and proclaim the word for His glory on Earth. No doubt, during the early stage of his ministry, he was on the right track and diligent to the things of God before his weakness and the source of his strength was revealed to his enemies through a woman. At this point, Samson missed the purpose and plan of God for his life because he began to trust in flesh and not in God alone. What made it worse was that he began to associate himself with the things of the world by indulging in worldly activities, and that is why God said, we Christians must put our trust in Him and Him alone and not in any man because man will definitely fail and disappoint you.

Have you ever asked yourself a question of how Samson discovered how the source of his strength to be his hair? The only way the strength of Samson was revealed to him was only by the help of the Holy Spirit through God for the sake of His glory alone to save His people from captivity in the hands of their enemies. Samson could not have known the source of his power if not for God who revealed it to him even when he was not yet even born.

John the Baptist was a saint and a man sent to come to the Earth by God primarily for a purpose which was to come soon for the coming of our Lord and to bear witness. I'm sure you will be wondering what kind of purpose this was for a man to come to the Earth from Heaven just to bear witness. John primarily came to pave and create a soft landing for the Light of the world to establish His kingdom on Earth according to the prophet Esaias. God had spiritually planned his coming and had made it to be so through His divine program and power.

John successfully achieved his purpose on Earth because he was dedicated and committed to the things of God that had sent him. He was humble and did not discriminate any one, whether you were a Jew or a Pharisees; he received everyone and preached the Gospel from the wilderness, proclaiming the coming of the One who is greater than him.

He was a honest man because he did not deny the fact that he is not the Messiah as recorded in the scripture even when people perceived him to be the Messiah, but through his open confession, he proclaimed the coming of our Lord. He also denied not his personality and purpose on Earth which of course was to bear witness. He said, "I am not the Christ" when the Jews sent priests and Levites from Jerusalem to ask him of who he really was.

> *And this is the record of John, when the when the Jews sent priests and Levites from Jerusalem to ask him, Who art thou? And he confessed, and denied not; but confessed, I am not the Christ. John 1:19–20 KJV*

He was a man that worked with God with all diligence by completely obeying God's instructions and referencing the Comforter in all he did while on Earth.

Having looked at Saint John, you will discover that he achieved his purpose on Earth before his physical life was taken by the king for an easy transition to eternal life where he came from. He knew he was not an ordinary man while on Earth because he allowed God to take preeminence in his affairs and ministry. I hope you have learnt a lesson from his life on Earth which is working according to how he lived by completely obeying God's words. You are not an ordinary man on Earth. There is something about you; please, it is important you know this as soon as possible.

The birth of our Lord Jesus was announced by angel Gabriel to a virgin who was the Earthly mother of Jesus Christ. His coming to Earth had been prophesied by different prophets according to the Old Testament. That was why the Jews were very curious to know who He really was. Although He was not accepted even while on Earth because they were expecting a god-man in the form of a man among them.

Our Lord Jesus Christ is the light of the world. He is the creator of the Earth, Universe, and the Heavens. He is before the creation of the Earth and was sent to Earth by God the Father primarily to humanity to bring eternal life, to destroy the works of the adversaries, and to possess the key of life and the gates of hell cannot prevail. Our Lord Jesus had a principle while fulfilling His purpose on Earth, and this principle was love. He brought this principal commandment for the total cleansing and reconciliation of mankind to God.

> *He came to unto his own, and his own received him not.*
> *John 1:11 KJV*

Our Lord did not allow this singular act of mankind to prevent Him from achieving His purpose on Earth; Rather, He continued diligently by proclaiming God the father and His authority on Earth. He has given us the power by the help of the Holy Spirit to live above sin, and he applied God's heavenly principle in His victorious mission on Earth.

Having looked at these men, you will discover that Jesus Christ and John the apostle achieved their purpose on Earth before departing to the world beyond simply because they applied God's principle while living in this world and placing the things of the spirit as priority. But Samson went astray when he began to take the things of this world and flesh more importantly than the things of God who had sent him. He allowed his status among men to becloud his primary purpose on Earth therefore giving the enemies entrance into his life which led to the exit of the presence of God in his life.

A critical study of some notable men in the history of human existence not recorded in the scripture, such as Martin Luther King Jr. and so many, will be briefly looked at. Martin's purpose on Earth was revealed to him through dream. He kept saying that he had a dream for unified American citizenship where there will be no discrimination of sex, color, age, and race. He stood on his ground not minding the danger it could cause him in achieving his purpose on Earth. He was focused, fearless, and dedicated to achieving this dream. You will agree with me that he is today celebrated for what he contributed to humanity and the prosperity of all American citizens. His purpose was made manifest today when the American people voted in a black man whose biological origin is Kenya to be the first black President of the USA, a great nation. Permit me to say that Martin was sent primarily to this Earth for the purpose of liberating the American people from some satanic chains in disguise. He will forever be remembered.

Nelson Mandela was a man from South Africa. He was one of the greatest African leaders that had ever existed. A critical look at his life will reveal that his mission on Earth was to primarily come and liberate black South Africans from bondage, discrimination, and slavery. This was demonstrated when he started his campaign against the white supremacy as regards giving the same opportunity and access to others on basic things of life. He was imprisoned for over two decades before God heard the cry of his people. His imprisonment did not prevent him from fulfilling his mission on Earth; rather it aggravated his spiritual man towards standing and focusing on achieving that which God sent him to do on Earth. His purpose on Earth was made manifest when the Holy Spirit gave him spiritual conviction of his mission as a teenager. He eventually became the first black president South Africa will ever have after so many years of slavery and bondage. This is a clear example of how Moses in the scripture worked with God to bring the children of Israel out of the land of captivity.

You are here on Earth for a purpose which must be accomplished, and one way you can receive and understand your divine purpose on Earth is through dreams. When we sleep, we know not where we are, for the real you is the spirit man which your body envelops. It is time you tell God to speak to you in your dream. I like you to know that a dream is a state of spiritual contact with spiritual things. We have all dreamed, and we know what it means when we see ourselves operating on the other side of life. Sometimes, a dream is the product of our imagination before we fall asleep. It is indisputable to also say thata dream is a spiritual communication with our spiritual being. But we need to know that life itself is a trinity comprising of love, education, and spirituality. It is your ability to equilibrate these that makes you a matured being, as we all know age is a number but wisdom is the principal thing. Life is spiritual for it is the spiritual that comes into manifestation in the physical. Nothing happens in this world by mistake for it is the activities in the spiritual realm that manifest in the physical, so it takes the spirit of God for you to understand what life is all about, and this could be made manifest through Him in your dream.

There was a true-life testimony of a man who had a dream. In his dream, God spoke to him to go and meet a wealthy man in a particular city with a description of the man's house, the name of the street where he lives, his name, complexion, physical structure, and every single detail. When this man woke up, he was terrified and confused but did not take the dream seriously and did not pray about it because he had not heard of such name before. Simultaneously, this rich man that same night had a dream that a particular man will come to meet him in his house and was instructed to help the man with what will cost him a lot. A description of the physical appearance of the poor man was also given to him. Months passed by and this rich man waited for the poor man and did not see him in order to confirm his dream. Suddenly one day, the poor man decided to give a trial to his dream by tracing where he was told to go in the dream. On getting to the house, he was marveled because it was a perfect description as revealed in the dream. He met some security guards at the gate of the rich man's house; after several questions of who he was looking for, he mentioned the rich man's name, and he was also asked if he had an appointment with their boss. He said no but he just decided to come and pay him a visit; it was exactly the rich man's house. Gripped with great confusion, the security men told him to wait outside for confirmation if the rich man was expecting him, and after some minutes, the security men told him to come in and that their boss had been expecting him for a long time.

When he met the rich man in his living room, he told him of the dream with great excitement. The rich man responded that he had the same dream the same night that he (the poor man) will come to him and he was instructed to bless him with what will cost him; this was how this poor man's life was changed from being poor to being a wealthy man in the society without working so hard for it. This is what we call God's divine visitation and blessing. It is inexplicable, but God can decide to do whatever that pleases Him for the sake of His children on Earth.

So many have told me how they saw themselves in their dreams been pursued by unknown persons or strange animals and were devoured; the next thing they say is that they are afraid. Whenever I here this, I feel so embarrassed, disappointed, and sorry for such folks not because of what had happened, but because these people perish for the lack of wisdom of the word of God.

The Lion is the king of all the animals in the forest, and anywhere the Lion shows up, other animals seek refuge. The problems most people have is that they fail to understand who they really are in God, and He is not happy with such people because they fail to operate in the level He has purposed them to operate in. You are supposed to be operating in a level that causes confusion in the camp of the enemy (Ephesians 6:10–18). You need to be bold like Jesus, the Lion of the tribe of Judah, to withstand all the works of the devourer and to tread upon serpents and scorpions. You need to come to the realization that there is someone in you that is greater than that which is in the world and who has all power both in heaven and on Earth for He will never leave nor forsake you in the days of trouble.

I was invited to a gathering when I was in the university and the man of God that came for this program talked about eating in dream, which so many people are used to in their dream. What really gave me joy that day was based on the fact that this preacher who is well known and filled with the Holy Ghost said if it would have been possible for these dream eaters to exchange their dream for his, he would be happy because he loves eating and so it would be better for his needs to be supplied through dream (food) as you know the heavenly food has not been tasted by anyone on Earth. If you do not have money to buy food, just pray to God and sleep; oh boy; wake up and you will be filled with heavenly food and you shall not hunger anymore. He will supply your needs according to His riches in glory by Christ Jesus, but you need to work and pray for Him to touch that situation of yours.

Those of you that eat in dream, do not be frightened; just thank God for supplying your need and praise Him. Do not be afraid because the moment you begin to nurse some element of fear, the enemy will capitalize on it and will use that to frighten you which will lead to your downfall in the things of God. All you need to do is to always pray and praise God. Get this straight, you need to be operating beyond men's understanding, and for this to work for you, it is by the help of the Holy Spirit who can reveal this to you sometimes through dreams.

He also talked about when he was a young man with family where he had no job. It was so bad that sometimes, he had no food to eat; this made him to always wait upon the Lord through fasting and prayers. During that period, there were some group of people that prepared demonic food and sacrifices for their gods that they always put it in front of his house. These sacrifices comprised of fish, turkey, egg, and some spiritual incursion. As a man waiting upon the Lord for breakthrough with no food to eat, he was tempted by these people, but he never knew his needs were supplied unknowingly by these people physically. So one day he prayed and waited upon the Lord for some days; as you know, man of God was very hungry and the first thing he saw on his doorstep was the assorted turkey laps, chicken, eggs, and so on as they have always done during their evil act. What he did amazed everyone in the gathering. He said that he looked to his right and left side and nobody was coming, so he took these things and ran inside. He said he cleaned, washed, and fried the turkey, chicken, and egg since he was the only one at home; he ate and was filled and gave thanks unto God, the supplier of his needs. The next day the same thing happened, and he did the same; the third day, man of God continued and was growing fat and fresh. As this was happening, he said they started noticing that his situation was getting better, so after some time, they stopped putting these things because the primary purpose for which they were put there had been defeated by this man of God. They started noticing an improvement in the life of the man of God. This led to an end in this spiritual war. At this point, the man of God started praying for this war to start over again. For within this period of time, he never bothered to buy meat for his meals. Folks, what a wonderful way to triumph over your enemies. You need to have a sound knowledge of the word of God to defeat the plans of the enemies in your life.

What I am trying to tell you is that you need to start operating beyond man's understanding because there is something in you greater than poison and any evil plan in your life as planned by the adversaries. All He needs is your faith and trust in Him. Get this right, I am not saying you should wake up one day and start going from one pole to the other looking for sacrifices to eat; the man of God was tempted by the devil and his needs were supplied by God through Christ Jesus and was activated by the help of the Holy Ghost and his faith and knowledge of the word of God.

As earlier said, your purpose on Earth can be revealed to you by God through your dream. Your future is in the hands of God who only can reveal this to you by communicating to you via your dream; a clear example to explicitly explain this is in the scripture.

I thank God for your life and what God is about to do concerning the revelation of your divine purpose in your life. We are all familiar with the story of Abraham who is the father of all nations; he was the father of faith who trusted God for his future and the life of his family. His name was changed from Abram to Abraham which means father of all nations, and this transformation of his life time came into manifestation through a dream which changed his entire life by the spirit of God. Before the Lord appeared to him, he was childless knowing not what the future holds for him. God knows what you are currently going through, and that is why you need to trust in God. Abraham was made fruitful, and God established his covenant with him and brought forth kings from his kindred. He found favor in the sight of God and yielded to God's word and direction (Genesis 12:1–4).

God gave Abraham a vision and he worked with God in all his ways. I want you to believe at this point that God is a God of vision and He is always there for you to achieve your dreams in life, but the problem is that, are you ready to work with God and also keep His commandments? Are you ready to go by His directions? God wants the best for you.

Joseph at the age of seventeen was the last child of Israel; he had favor in the sight of God and men. He had a dream which signified greatness ahead of him. God revealed his future to him through dream in order for him to be ready for the great task ahead of him. Looking at Abraham's life, I noticed something which is significantly different from that of Joseph. When this revelation was given to him, he kept it to himself and never discussed it with anyone. What he did was take all his belongings and went away to a place called the promise land for which God had appointed him to be. It is apparent that maturity took its place in the life of Abraham because he never discussed it with his brethren knowing fully well the crafty nature of men but obeyed the voice of the Lord and left. But Joseph being a little boy did not really understand what God was trying to pass across to him. He shared it with his brethren who were already jealous of him just because he had favor in the sight of God and men, especially his father.

I must tell you that some people are dream killers; these people do not want the best for you; they derive joy seeing that you do not achieve your divine purpose on Earth, and they would go at length to see that you do not prosper in all you do. Please, I am telling you that you need God's direction in all you do. If you really observe Joseph being a little boy, he was not working according to the instructions of the spirit of God, but God decided to use his situation to bring to manifestation His purpose for Joseph's creation to the amazement of his enemies.

You need to really work with God; He knows what is best for you. When you have a dream, think it, see it, visualize it, team it by consulting the Holy Spirit, and achieve your dreams. The question now is who to team these dreams with. What I can tell you is that you need the comforter in such situation to lead and direct you (John 10:10).

Joseph's brethren acted as the adversaries to the achievement of his dreams, but God acted on their plan to fulfilling His purpose for his life. You will agree with me that they ignorantly acted as a channel for his purpose to be fulfilled on Earth. He was sold to the Ishmaelite and was taken to Egypt where God had purposed, prepared, and planned for him to rule for the period he was destined to live. In the process of heading toward his purpose, he had problems that led him to prison which was an avenue for achieving his destiny as a ruler in the land of Egypt. Listen carefully, no matter what you are passing through, your Heavenly Father is aware. In order to achieve this, God gave him wisdom to interpret dreams which led him to become the ruler of Egypt and the second-in-command. The devil thought he had succeeded in killing his dreams, but he had favor and achieved his purpose on Earth and his brethren bowed before him as revealed in his dream (Genesis 37:5, 9).

I know you have dreams, visions, and aspirations; the most important thing is for you to know how to achieve these dreams, and you can only know this by the help of the Holy Ghost. Do you know that vision is a light that shines forth to lead and direct your path? Jesus Christ is a vision supplier (John 1:4–5).

Do you have dreams and visions that seem impossible in your heart? Or are you discouraged by what is happening in your life? You should not be weary for God is the ultimate dream achiever. You have only one means to achieve your dreams and aspirations in life; all you need is the wisdom from God to interpret your dream and His revelation of the right channel of achieving your dreams on Earth. Do not forget to go to Him in praise and worship with prayers and commit everything in the hands of God; also, always ask for the power of God. After this, I promise you that you will receive the Holy Ghost who will help you bear witness unto the uttermost part of the Earth and you will testify of His goodness in your life.

Do you have a dream and things seem not to work well? I admonish you to go back and seek the face of God because you might have a wrong dream. I want you to now see yourself as a goal achiever and one who has come to the realization of the understanding of His revelation of His purpose for your life, having understood that you are already becoming what God wants you to become by His grace and favor in your life. All you need now is help from the Holy Spirit and wisdom to carry on with your goal to achieving His divine purpose for which you were created. He cares for you and wants the best for you. Be positive in all you do, think positive, live positive, love your neighbors as you love yourself, and always live a life that is above sin because you bear inside of you the nature of God.

At this point, the purpose for your creation would be unveiled to you even as you come to the realization of His purpose for your life. All you need now is to avoid every distraction and devote your heart to the revelation that is about to be passed on to you. In the next chapter lies His divine purpose for your life and His desires for man as revealed in the scripture. God bless you even as you give your heart to His word for breakthrough and blessing in all you do. Amen.

CHAPTER FOUR

GOD'S DIVINE PURPOSE FOR CREATING MAN

And God blessed them, and God said unto them, be fruitful, and multiply, and replenish the earth, and subdue it: and have dominion over the fish of the sea, and over the fowl of the air, and over every living thing that moveth upon the earth. Genesis 1:28 KJV

I want to thank God for your life and your future; this is because He has given you the opportunity to be a partaker of His blessings. What I would like you to do now is to answer these questions within your spirit man. Have you ever sat down in your closet anytime of your life and reflected on the main reason or purpose why you were created? Are you created to fill up the empty space on this planet Earth? I think it is pertinent to know why you were created biblically. Listen, you are not created for the sake of existing, but there is a specific purpose for your existence on this planet. Looking at your life, what impact have you made on the lives around you? Ask yourself, what impact have I made to strategically transform lives positively? What is my purpose on Earth? These are some of the questions that you will find answers soon.

You are God's chosen, the apple of His eyes; you are created in the image and likeness of God; you are a house set on a hill that cannot be hidden. I want you to know that you are a blessing to your generation. Do you know that you are blessed? It can only take some time as the case may be and sometimes expedient which depends on God's plan for your blessings to manifest. It is the manifestation of the spiritual blessing that reflects in the physical. Start telling yourself that you are a blessing defined and personified and you will be a blessing to your generation.

If you extensively meditate on the scripture and put yourself in that position as mandated by our Heavenly Father to His chosen people, it says God has bestowed on you blessings from the inner treasures of the heavenly places, and He pronounced five words to entirely take care of your life before you were born while in the womb. Scripturally, there are five major purposes for the creation of man as stated by God in the beginning of the world, and these words were spoken unto you when you were created through the breath He breathed into you (His Spirit) in the process of your creation. He said, "my son, my daughter:

- **BE FRUITFUL**
- **MULTIPLY**
- **REPLENISH**
- **SUBDUE**
- **DOMINATE.**

At this point we will extensively explain what our Heavenly Father meant when He spoke these words in your life. Henceforth, you have responsibility and mandate of the following:

FRUITFULNESS

In the beginning of creation, the spirit of the living God walked on the surface of the deep and He saw that everything was perfect as planned. This signifies that when you were created, you were made perfect by the spirit of God. The first word our God pronounced upon your life was to "be fruitful" which means that fruitfulness is significantly part of your destiny. Imagine from a deep sleep, the first word you heard loud and clear from someone was "be fruitful"; how would you feel? The word of God is a source of hope and strength to any man to actively carry on with daily routine of life. You need Christ for you to be fruitful in all your endeavors in life.

> *I am the vine, ye are the branches: He that abideth in me, and I in him, the same bringeth forth much fruit; for without me ye can do nothing. John 15:5 KJV*

Every living soul on Earth has a life cycle and a primary source that sustains its existence. That is why from the last statement, you need Him to be alive and to also make a significant success in all you do. He is the vine and without the vine, the branches cannot produce good fruit. The scripture says that life in Christ is the hope of all glory. You are destined to be fruitful because it is your final destination in your race of this life.

> *This book of the law shall not depart out of thy mouth; but thou shalt meditate therein day and night, that thou mayest observe to do according to all that is written therein: for then thou shalt make thy way prosperous, and then thou shalt have good success. Joshua 1:8 KJV*

Eh! Folks, do you know that courage, love, and confidence are a vital key to success? When you are fruitful, it takes you into the supernatural which culminates into becoming successful in life. You can only be fruitful by the word of God which is Jesus Christ. The Holy Ghost in your life will direct you on the right path of success. You need to meditate on the word of God and His commandment which is love, for this is the only criteria for your success in life and not only meditating but living according to His will. When you cultivate the habit of working with the Holy Spirit, you will start swimming in an ocean of success. Do you know that success is the easiest thing to achieve on Earth? The human philosophy or perception of success can be seen as:

Hard Work + Focus + Dedication + Opportunity = Success

You need to know that there is a big difference between God's kind of success and how the world tends to define success. What is defined above is what I used to believe to be success. As can be seen above, it is hard work in whatever you do, absolute submission in whatever you find yourself doing. You also need to be focused in your life in addition to your aspirations of life because vision brings focus and focus gives you a pathway to success. You need to also be dedicated in whatever you do, and dedication to your plans with all tenacity speeds up the level and rate of success. Opportunity is also an important aspect of success, and this is where the human understanding fails to recognize the importance of grace which is an unmerited favor from God.

The above cannot be disputed but there is a clear difference between good success and success. Good success does not have limit. Good success is the Godly kind of success, while success is the human philosophy of what success is all about. There is a statement that says "the sky is your limit" which can be seen to a reasonable extent as success. But good success can also be said to be the "sky is your stepping stone, not your limit"; what this means is that when you get to the sky, that is when the race for your success manifests itself in a positive direction.

The Godly kind of success can be defined as:

Hard Work + Focus + Dedication + Prayer + Grace = Good Success

The last word has been completely omitted by many people who call themselves successful men and women in our present day. Grace is a state of operating in the supernatural atmosphere of God's intervention in a man's life. It is a state of effortless input with an outstanding output in any situation a man faces. Going by the above definition of a good success, it is revealed that when a man is hardworking and puts in 100% concentration in what he is trying to achieve with dedication backed with consistent prayers, it gives such a man success. But when God is given an open invitation into your situation, grace accompanies our Creator. He is our God who will come into that situation with an envelope of grace which you do not merit.

When Jesus Christ said in the Saint John Gospel that it is impossible for a camel to pass through the eye of a needle than for a rich man to enter into the kingdom of God, Jesus Christ did not mean every rich man would not enter into the kingdom of His Father, but He was trying to say that so many people do not have Christ in their lives and feel they can live freely but not knowing it is the highest risk anyone can ever take in his or her entire lifetime.

> *If a man abide not in me, he is cast forth as a branch, and is withered; and men gather them, and cast them into the fire, and they are burned. John 15:6 KJV*

You need grace for good success. Good success does not come but only by Christ Jesus who is the author and finisher of your faith. He further said in verse seven of that same chapter that "if ye abide in me and my words abide in you, ye shall ask what ye will and it shall be done unto you."

You need to abide in the knowledge of God's word for it is a stream where the rivers of joy proceed from. The wisdom you need to be able to go about achieving good success would be revealed to you by the anointing of the Holy Ghost. When you abide in Him, He will make His abode in you, and when this is done, you will start operating under the umbrella of the Almighty God who will direct your path toward peace, good success, and joy in your life; isn't that great? When a man is operating under the guiding principle of his creation, some of the attributes of his life will be enveloped with the following:

Prosperity

And he shall be like a tree planted by the rivers of water that bringeth forth his fruit in his season, his leaf also shall not wither; and whatsoever he doeth shall prosper. Psalm 1:3 KJV

Prosperity is a state of being a successful person in all areas of life most especially when a man according to human understanding is financially independent or rather, say, can afford whatever he wishes for. Do you know that when you are in a state of prosperity, it means that you are in a state of fruitfulness? When you are operating in a fruitful situation, it means you are prospering, and when you are operating in this realm, it means you do not lack in any form. In this state of life, your needs are supplied by the grace of God. Our God is a prosperous God and the Bible said:

But my God shall supply all your need according to his riches in glory by Christ Jesus. Philippians 4:19 KJV

I do not know the level you are currently operating in at the moment; you might be operating in the level of prosperity; if so, it is pertinent you thank God for His faithfulness and provision in your life. If you have not started operating in that level of prosperity, then there is a great chance for you. What you need is wisdom to start operating in the realm. God created the Heaven and Earth by His wisdom, and that wisdom He has bestowed in you. Ask yourself, may be you have not utilized efficiently that potential in you that is needed to take you to the greater height of working in prosperity.

The only difference between you and that man is grace. Becoming prosperous starts from an idea which culminates into reality depending on what you believe in. It also starts from a moment of drastic change in your mental state of mind. What I mean is that you can start operating in the realm of prosperity in just one second; all you need is God's divine grace and favor which come into manifestation when you are operating in the heavenly ideas beyond human understanding by the supernatural power of the Almighty God. You need this special substance to be prosperous.

Someone will say we all need divine connection in our lives for breakthrough. Yes, I quite agree, but it is necessary to understand that divine connection is a state of operating under the influence of the direction of the Holy Ghost. This is because He knows what you need, how to get what you require to achieve it, and how to divinely connect you. When you are divinely connected, it means you are divinely favored, and divine favor crystallizes into divine success. Divine favor has a lot to do with your level of prosperity; when you are in a state of God's favor, your life will always be filled with happiness of mind and body, blessings, peace, and love. Do not be afraid about what the future holds for you; your future is so bright because it is in the hand of the Lord who knows you and who also wants the best for you.

> *But the very hairs of your head are all numbered fear ye not therefore, ye are of more value than many sparrows. Matthew 10:30–31 KJV*

He knows you more than you know yourself, and He wants the best for you in all your future endeavors. Do you know one thing that sets so many backward? It will interest you to know that a man's inability to believe in the word of God has a negative multiplier impact, and this can practically set a man toward an opposite direction of God's plan for his life. You need to change your philosophy of what life is all about. You need to start prophesying positively into your life. It is time you talk like that person who you really are. The truth of the matter is that your life from henceforth has taken a new shape. I know you have the power to talk to that situation. Start telling yourself and prophesying that "I refuse to be poor, I refuse to be confused about life, I refuse to feel inferior, and I refuse to lack," for God has told you to be fruitful and His words are "yeah and amen"; His word cannot go void until it accomplishes that which it is assigned to; you are born to be fruitful and to prosper.

Have you been trying to execute a project and it seems not to be going on the way you want it, or are you the type of a person who has been operating below the level where you want to see yourself? All you need is to start seeing yourself in the nearest future operating in your desired realm. My God is not a God that sleeps nor slumbers; He will meet you at the point of your needs and will always be there for you all the time; isn't that wonderful? All you have to do is call upon Him. I admonish you to cleave unto Him and trust in Him for that thing you want. There is nothing impossible for Him to do (Mathew 11:28).

Career Pursuit

> *For wisdom is a defense and money is a defense; but the excellency of knowledge is, that wisdom giveth life to them that have it. Ecclesiastes 7:12 KJV*

When God created you, He enveloped you with His own kind of wisdom to excel in your chosen career or profession. That is why when others seem not to be doing well or when others are failing, you are succeeding and when others are not favored, you are operating under the influence of grace. Knowledge is the information or experience we derive from a particular task we were once involved in either through education or personal research, while wisdom is your ability to apply this knowledge you have to an empirical situation. There are some facts you need to understand about wisdom, and these are based on the obvious truth that there is a big difference between God's kind of wisdom and man's wisdom. God's kind of wisdom is that which we possess as Christians that enables us to do things that are beyond man's comprehension. God's kind of wisdom directs us and teaches us "all things," not "some things," and the spirit searches all things, the deep things of God thus say the scripture. He has revealed to us things that cannot be discerned by the natural man which is the vitamin for our fruitfulness in all aspect of our lives.

The natural man's wisdom is wisdom that originates from human flesh, and it is foolishness with God (1 Corinthians 3:19). It is the general belief of this world that gray hair is a sign of old age and accumulation of wisdom. It is said that the words of the old are wise and based on wisdom. It is indisputable, but this wisdom is entirely different from the wisdom we the chosen generation exhibit on Earth. We act and work like Christ operating under the influence of the Spirit of God as we bear on us the mark of Christ.

Are you a professional in your field? You might be an economist, engineer, philosopher, lawyer, banker, doctor, and so on. How is your specialization going with you? Having that experience in such profession, it means you have knowledge on such field, but the question now is, have you been able to empirically apply this knowledge which helps you exhibit wisdom? You really need the wisdom of the Holy Spirit as you can do nothing without God's kind of wisdom which you can only get by working closely with Him for He has given you the ability and power to do things in your field which someone else cannot do easily because such wisdom is going to inspire you to do greater things without stress.

Are you a student that is finding it hard to acquire knowledge in some of the various disciplines? You need to really search your heart and the things you do, because those activities you are involved in might have grieved the Holy Spirit which has eventually led to His departure from your life, and without Him you cannot excel in your academic work. But the good news is that you can still reconcile with Him; all you have to do is trust in the Lord with your heart and acknowledge Him in your life for it is the only criteria that can take you to the greatest height in your academic work.

Be fruitful in all you do. He has spoken this word into your life; this is a word from your creator because there is this innate ability bestowed upon you that causes you to be fruitful in your pursuit, and not until you discover this fact, you might not produce a more efficient result which will make you to be less productive in that field you found yourself. You need to start activating the word of God concerning your career; you also have to seek God for a Godly kind of wisdom that will strengthen you to do all things by His words for therein are power, strength, innovation, invention, and discovery beyond human imagination. He is going to distinct you from others because you are unique; you no longer operate under the influence of this world but under the influence and direction of the Holy Spirit who will teach you all things to come.

> *I can do all things through Christ which strengtheneth me. Philippians 4:13 KJV*

Folks, wow this is interesting, can you imagine that? You can do "all things," not some things," by Christ who is your strength, for Christ in you is the hope of glory. Do you know that Christ in you activates God's wisdom which makes you think, talk, walk, and live like Christ? Be fruitful in your career and your future endeavors.

Marital Bliss

> *And said, for this cause shall a man leave father and mother, and shall cleave to his wife and they twain shall be one flesh? Wherefore they are no more twain but shall be one flesh. What therefore God hath joined together, let not man put asunder. Matthew 19:5–6 KJV*

According to this scripture, God ordained marriage in such a way that two different persons that are both female and male who have true love for one another spiritually become one. In the book of Genesis 2:22– 25, it was revealed that a woman was made out of a man's ribs and this rib was used by God to create a woman. He that finds a good wife finds blessings and favor in the sight of God. God has created you to have marital bliss and to also use this as a point of contact to glorify His name. He said be fruitful in your marriage. Get this straight folks, you can never be barren. There shall be none barren in the land, thus says the Lord; He has pronounced these blessings in your life which automatically means that there is no way you can be barren. You shall bear children and your children shall be greater than you and also be a blessing to their generation; thus sayeth the word of God to you. You were created for fruitfulness so you cannot be incapacitated in any area of your marriage.

Are you married? If yes, how is your marriage? Is your marriage facing trials and hard times? I have good news for you. Do you know that "there is nothing impossible for God to do?" There are times God works in ways that are beyond human comprehension. Do you know that sometimes we seem to ask God different and diverse questions as regards our marital problems and yet we cannot find answers basically because of our distant relationship with our creator? There are several divorces, breakups, and infirmities in different homes, and close to eighty percent of these are as a result of the absence of the Holy Spirit in such homes. There are times God deliberately turns His back at us in that our precarious situation for good and to also test if you are a faithful child. I do not know how many years you have been waiting upon the Lord for some new things in your marriage. The truth is that you will definitely experience the hand of God in your marriage today. If you strongly believe these words, say amen in your spirit and watch what will start happening in your marriage.

Come to think of it, do you know that you are a seed from Abraham? Do you remember God's promise to Abraham's seed? You will bear children and your children will be a blessing to nations and kings and princes shall spring up from your lineage, but there is something very important for this to manifest; it is so easy and simple because it just takes for you to put in your faith and trust in the Lord. You might be there without a womb or expecting God to heal you; all you have to know is that all things work together for good to those that trust and believe in God. Start seeing yourself as a father, mother, or parent by faith. I do not know what the doctor has told you about your situation; doctors are not God, and they cannot create any part in your body and can't say yes when the Lord has not spoken. Whose report would you believe? And who told you that you cannot bear children? Get this: "Nothing is impossible for God to do." Start shopping for your newborn baby because heaven is dispatching your children for greatness

But the very hairs of your head are all numbered.
Matthew 10:30 KJV

There are sometimes God will deliberately delay some marriages from having children as at when they expect for some particular reasons. You might want to have children so fast in your own way by making sure that you bear children, but this might be different from the purpose of God in your marriage. Sometimes God could do this to raise up a great child from you that will bring down His glory from heaven. There are children that are destined to arrive here on Earth at a particular season based on God's divine program for His glory. Closely looking at the scripture, I noticed that God purposely delayed some marital fruitfulness basically in order to make manifest an outstanding mark in the history of human existence for the sake of our blessing. A further look at Abraham, Sarah, and their maid Hagar, it would be observed that both Abraham and Sarah were so conscious and were in a hurry to have children, but it was contrary to God's purpose for their marriage. God was preserving Sarah for greatness ahead of them. God had an appointed time for her to bear a child, and He did this for the manifestation of His word. Do you know that she had to hire Hagar to bear for her husband a child which led to losing her respect in the sight of Hagar? Moreover, Hagar's son was destined to be a wild man and will be against every man and every man against him. But patiently, both Abraham and Sarah were of age, and at the appointed time, they had a son called Isaac, and God established his covenant with him.

Also, looking at Zechariah the priest and Elizabeth, both stricken in age, they begat John the Baptist who was and is still a blessing to many lives according to the scriptures. John the Baptist was God sent; he had a purpose on Earth, and one of the eminent purposes was to come and prepare the ground for the coming of our Lord Jesus Christ, and he had the spirit of God in him who directed his path and his purpose on Earth. He fulfilled his purpose on Earth by leading many to Christ and was a blessing to many lives during his ministry on Earth.

Is there anything too hard for the Lord? For at the appointed time He will return unto thee, according to the time of life, and you shall have a child who has a covenant with God for greatness, particular purpose, and achievement, thus saith the Lord. As I have said earlier, you need to have faith in the Lord, trust in Him, believe Him, and Worship him because you shall in this time next season bear a child who will be greater than you and who shall be a blessing to his or her generation. You need to be watchful for the miraculous work of the Lord in your life as regard your marriage; you will never lack in your marriage, for it is possible to please God with your faith. As you wait upon the Lord for the appointed time, you will always be filled with the blessing and anointing of God in your life in Jesus' name.

Good health

> *Beloved, I wish above all things that thou mayest prosper and be in health, even as thy soul prospereth. 3 John 1:2 KJV*

God has a wish, purpose, and thought toward you. He said He wish above "all things," not "some things." Please get these words, "all things," meaning, His greatest wish is for you to prosper in all ramification of life and be in good health. The process of human creation involves a creative process, and this process involves a singular act which God applied, and this is the breath that was placed into you. He breathes into your life, the breath of fruitfulness which brings good health of mind and body into your soul. He loves you so much, and that is why He took away your burdens, sicknesses, diseases, deformities, anxieties, and other negative things pertaining to your life. He made you above all forms of unfortunate life's circumstances. The only means you can be destroyed by the adversary is through fear (Hebrews 2:15). The devil does not have the power of death; he has been overthrown by the blood of the lamb. The thoughts of our Lord toward you are not of evil but good to give you that expected end.

When our Lord Jesus died on the cross of Calvary, we Christians, the chosen ones, died with Him. When He was buried, we were buried with Him. When He resurrected, we were there with Him. When He went to hell, we were with Him. When He defeated the devil, we were with Him. Isn't that great? You need to know that you are Christ-like. You carry the mark of the living God; this is why He was made to carry your sickness and this He did for your sake. Do not limit yourself to things that have been sorted out by the living God, and not until you come to this realization, you might not work in the direction of the Almighty. I do not know the report that has been given to you by the doctors; all I know is this:

> *But he was wounded for our transgressions, he was bruised for our iniquities: the chastisement of our peace was upon him; and with his stripes we are healed. Isaiah 53:5 KJV*

The word of God cannot lie. It is only when you come to the realization of the limelight of His word and start operating in the knowledge of the Holy Spirit you might continue to work under the counsel of the ungodly. Do you know what? I have never for one day believed all those names or so-called diseases that the present medical professionals call them. They make the report so polished to make it look like one very important and scary disease. All you need is to apply God's own kind of principle to your life. Whose report will you believe? I admonish that you believe the report of the Most High God.

> *And said, if thou wilt diligently hearken to the voice of the Lord thy God, and wilt do that which is right in his sight, and wilt give ear to his commandments, and keep all his status, I will put none of these diseases upon thee, which I have brought upon the Egyptians: for I am the LORD that healeth thee. Exodus 15:26 KJV*

Our Heavenly Father led the children of Israel out of the land of bondage, and He also blessed them on their way to the promise land; He gave them all they needed in the course of their journey. His word for your life today is that you are healed, because He is the God that healeth thee. He said if you hearken unto the voice of the Almighty and will obey His words, He would take away from thee all of these diseases among you. His word is a light unto your path and a lamb unto your feet. Do not be surprised when you hear men of God say that ever since they gave their lives to Jesus Christ, they had never visited the hospital nor had headache.

The fact of life is that the breath of God in you as a child of God causes all forms of infirmities to give way. All you have to do is to recognize Him as vital to your existence, and once you do, He takes charge of your life which helps you to stop operating under the influence of the flesh but by the Holy Spirit who will keep you and take away sickness out of thee. When this happens, your mortal body would be vitalized which makes you a supernatural being on Earth operating above the devices of the adversaries. Living in such a situation makes you bear the mark of Christ, and the Holy Spirit will continue to dwell in you because you are now His temple. Sickness cannot dwell inside of you; diseases cannot dwell inside of you; anxiety cannot dwell inside of you; and poverty cannot dwell inside of you, for when they see the blood, they would pass over you. You are now a living testimony of the word of God. The Lord does not and will never wish anyone to have health disorder; His wish for you is to be in good health and have a sound mind of body.

Having read through the scripture, I noticed that one major focus of our Lord Jesus Christ during His time on Earth was miracles. He saw pains being inflicted upon so many people around Him by diseases and sicknesses, and that is one reason why He came to redeem man from every sickness of life. He came so that you might have good health, and one very unique feature about Jesus Christ was that He was very quick to having compassion on the multitude whenever He saw them running after Him.

A vivid scenario was the woman with the issue of blood for twelve years. She proposed in her heart that the very moment when she comes in contact with Jesus, with a mind full of desires and faith in God, she will be healed of her disease; immediately she was made whole by just touching our Lord's garment. The very moment you come in contact with Jesus Christ, you will not be the same old person you have always been. You will become a new creature. For old things have passed away, behold you have become new.

Reading through the gospel, I discovered that during our Lord Jesus

Christ's time on Earth, He worked perfectly with the Holy Spirit, and that was why He lived above sin. He did not and could not struggle with sin for the Holy Ghost was with Him to teach, direct, and keep Him in all His ways; that was why He said not until I go, the Comforter will not come. So many people are asking questions about the Holy Ghost and where He is; anytime I hear this, I feel in my spirit that such statement comes from the flesh. They forget that He has come in spirit and not flesh.

Our Lord was filled with the Holy Spirit from the moment He was baptized by John the Baptist. This was made manifest when the Holy Ghost descended upon our Lord as a dove, and from thence the purpose for His coming started unfolding and He began His ministry and purpose on Earth. When the woman with the issue of blood touched Him, it was ministered unto Him by the Holy Spirit through divine power that something had happened in the spiritual realm. Our Lord is God and He lived on Earth as a human being.

If you have the Holy Spirit, it means you have virtue inside of you that is ready to fight against any diseases or sicknesses that comes your way. Your body is now equipped with vaccine to fight against any form of diseases that is contrary to the well-being of your body. These are vaccines that help you operate in a state of grace. Have you ever seen in the scripture where it is written that our Lord Jesus was ill? God forbid, it is impossible. He came and healed the sick, broken hearted, the leper, the blind, and those oppressed and possessed by the devil. Brethren, you are God's chosen ones and your body is the temple of the Holy Spirit which makes you a supernatural person on Earth through Christ. You cannot be sick because He bore all your infirmities on the cross. I must tell you that the doctor's report shouldn't petrify it.

MULTIPLY

One day while I was discussing with a friend, he told me that he was planning on starting a business. He then told me that there was someone he would like to see before he embarks on this business because he knows apparently that this person he is in search of knows about this particular business and how to go about starting it. Could you believe that I had been nurturing this same business in my heart and deliberating on how to go about it? Immediately what came to my mind was planning. Anyone who fails to plan plans to fail. What really amazed me was that we had the same mindset in terms of the business idea and also thinking toward a particular direction in line with it.

There are times when God will put a particular idea in your mind and, at the same time, He would send someone to help you acquire all you need to carry out the special plan He has for you. From my discussions with this friend, I realized that he was going to be of great help to me in the course of the business which made me to start thinking closely in line with him on how to go about things. God said I will never forsake you nor leave you in times of trouble or difficulty; He would help you plan for the things that are yet to come, and He will give you ideas and strategies to carry out this proposed idea He has given unto you.

When you were created, He spoke into your life, saying, "go and multiply." To multiply means to increase in all aspects of your life which will give you express passport to excel at whatever you do. You are born to multiply and not remain static; you cannot diminish but rather increase in all you do. In life, there is a guiding principle of sowing and reaping, just like the process flow involved in the natural cultivation of a farm, so it also applies as a time to sow and a time to reap; the same applies to the process flow involved in human existence on Earth. Our God is still in the business and active in the area of multiplication of your seeds for greatness in your life.

I need you to know that it is the wish of God that your seeds be multiplied and the works of your hands be blessed. He has separated you from the people of the Earth to inherit what He has packaged for you, and He has given you the authority to possess your possessions. He said, "Come let us reason together and put me into the remembrance of my words concerning your life." God has a word for your life, and this word will never go void until it accomplishes that which has been spoken pertaining what He has said. You need to put into activation the word of God in your life; His word is the only road to salvation and eternal life which has been prepared for you.

I: Savings

> *The wise man saves for the future, but the foolish man spends whatever he gets. Proverbs 21:5 TLB*

Your finance is a determinant of future financial freedom in relative terms. Your decision today concerning the effective utilization of the resources you have has a multiplier effect on your future. The decision you take now has either a positive or negative multiplier effect on how your tomorrow will be. Decision-making is one very vital and necessary aspect of a man's life, and the decision(s) we make is (are) based on choice and life itself is all about choice. You can take a decision that will affect you for the rest of your life either positively or negatively, and this you can only take efficaciously when you diligently seek the face of God in whatever you do.

Savings is the proportion of your income left either in the bank or an alternate safekeeping after the deduction of personal income tax. According to a sample primary data research I carried out, it was discovered and concluded that the average person saves less than one percent of his income and over sixty percent of adults have no savings whatsoever especially considering the global issues currently facing household across continents. Many people do not have savings or do not save some proportion out of their income, and this portrays what the Bible calls a foolish man. When you do not save, it means you are not securing your future, and when your future is not secured, it means you have no future, and a man without a future is like a dead man. You need a steady ploy back of your return and save some of your resources; if you do not save, it means you are not a good Christian, for a good Christian, no matter how small, must save for the later day.

There is a treasure to be desired and oil in the dwelling of the wise; but a foolish man spendeth it up. Proverbs 21:20 KJV

God has rightly commanded us to save some portion of our income. Scripturally, if we fail to live by this principle, we are disobeying God's word. When you save, it means you are depriving yourself of some needs or wants for the unseen, unperceived, unexpected future financial needs. When you save, you are increasing your income because on this savings, you will earn interest if saved in a bank which will help you plan for the future. Below is a mathematical representation of how everyone spends his or her daily, weekly, and monthly income:

$Y = S + I + X$
Y represents our income.
S represents savings.
I represents investment.
X represents other expenditure.
We can also represent our saving as: $S = Y - I - X$

It is a known fact that our income is limited, while the resources that are available to us are limited to meet these needs that are unlimited. When we earn or receive income or money from service rendered, it is expected that we either save some portion, invest some, or spend the rest to meet some of our needs such as paying our bills and insurance and giving to our dependents or the poor (Acts 20:35).

We all have our heart desires and always pray to our Heavenly Father to grant it to us. One thing we fail to realize is that we have gone contrary to the will of God for our lives. The scripture says that the foolish spends every income realized and does not save a portion for the rainy day(s). When this happens, we often question God and feel disappointed. Have you forgotten that He said save and save as much as you can? I am sure you are familiar with Joseph and how he was able to withstand and plan for the famine period in Egypt. This is how God wants you to live your life. Joseph's lifestyle is a vivid example on how to live a purposeful driven life. You need to commit your finance into the hands of God and also tell Him to direct your finances.

God wants you to live a decent and progressive life. When you cultivate the habit of saving, you will start operating in the realm God wants you to be operating. Consistent savings from your income helps create a decent and fruitful life. When you save, lack will be far from you at all times; it helps you become a giver and not at the receiving end. If you have not consciously cultivated the habit of saving, I encourage you to start today. You can draw up a plan on how you will protect your future; decide on a particular percentage from your daily, weekly, or monthly income you want to be saving. It is very important you do this because it will help you plan for the future. I am optimistic and convinced in my spirit that by virtue of the fact that you have come in contact with this book, your life will never be the same again. You are wise and not foolish because you are a child of God. Say to yourself: I am wise because I am in a team that believes in saving!

II: Investment

> *Steady plodding brings prosperity; hasty speculation brings poverty. Proverbs 21:5 TLB*

$$I = Y - S - X$$

One of the basic and important fundamental principles of investment you need to practice in order to become a successful investor is for you to spend less than you earn and save and invest what you have acquired through this principle over a period of time. Just take time out to study the end result of anyone around you that spends more than what he or she earns, and see the final outcome of the person's life. It is impossible for such an individual to prosper as the Bible rightly said it is penury that will be the end result of such an individual. You have the opportunity to change and follow the right path to success. I have heard some people say that they do not know what to invest in, or rather they do not have knowledge on the right business to invest in; I must tell you that it is lack of knowledge that will make a man perish.

We have several investment analysts on any kind of business or investment no matter how little your funds are; it is important you seek their advice and services for positive growth in your income. It is a principle of life: he who sow must surely reap. You cannot sow corn and expect to reap cassava; you have to invest in your future and spiritually sow into the future of your eternal life. You need to constantly inculcate the habit of investing your resources to protect your future and also increase the level of your future savings. The more you invest in a clearly defined business, the more you have prosperity in the nearest future.

> *There be four things which are little upon the earth, but they are exceedingly wise: The ants are a people not strong, yet they prepare their meat in the summer. Proverbs 30:24, 25 KJV*

Wow! I love the way the Bible described the ants; imagine the level of their wisdom. One amazing fact about ants is that they are so fragile but highly intelligent. If the scripture can describe ants in such a pleasant and highly esteemed manner, how much more you that is created in the image and likeness of our Heavenly Father. You are much more precious and relevant on this Earth which belongs to our God. Kindly take out time to draw up a comprehensive plan on how to secure your future through investing in a viable and lucrative business.

> *There is another serious problem I have seen everywhere—savings are put into risky investment that turn sour, and soon there is nothing left to pass on to one's son. The man who speculates is soon back to where he began with nothing. Ecclesiastes 5:13–15 TLB*

From the scripture above, it is apparent that so many people work and operate without the help of the Holy Spirit. You cannot be successful without the help of the Holy Ghost. He is there to teach you and direct your path on what to and not invest in. So many people have succeeded in trading off their future riches simply because they imagine doing it alone without the help of God. When you have the Spirit of God, He will teach and lecture you on what to invest in spiritually, which subconsciously will be made manifest in the physical without your knowledge.

I believe you have heard of or rather seen so many wealthy or rich men and women that went down the ladder in life because they refused to work with the comforter (Holy Ghost). In most cases, such people think it is by their power that they got to where they are, but not knowing that it is by His grace that we are not consumed by our adversaries. A clear example is Job in the scripture. I believe you are familiar with the story; just within some hours, his life was turned around negatively simply because God allowed it to happen to test his faith and trust in Him. The adversaries can reap you off your entire life savings if you are not on the Lord's side. Protect your future by committing it in the hands of God. You are a conqueror and victorious by the help of the Holy Spirit who will teach you to invest in the right kind of investment.

> *Give a portion to seven, and also to eight; for thou knowest not what evil shall be upon the earth. Ecclesiastes 11:2 KJV*

The importance of diversification of resources cannot be overemphasized. From the days of our fathers based on the scriptures, the secret of operating in abundance has been given to us. As Christians, we must and have to diversify our limited resources. What I am saying in essence is that you need to apply God's kind of wisdom when investing. Multiple streams of income are better than a single source of income. When your income inflows are in multiple forms, it helps in acquiring more resources for you to take care of your needs and that of others' around you. He will supply all your needs according to His riches in Glory through Christ Jesus. God will not come down from heaven to supply your needs, but He will place in you wisdom to make wealth and to provide for your household and dependent(s) and also make you a blessing to your generation.

You do not have to throw all your eggs into one basket; you have to diversify your limited resources for safety purposes. It is better for a man to keep his money in different sources of returns basically in case of any future misfortune especially as a result of diverse negative economic process flow. It is a risk for you to keep the whole sum of your limited resources in a particular investment considering the level of volatility in the world economy. Now tell me, if such an investment happens to liquidate or be destroyed by some uncontrollable disaster(s), what would become of you and the whole money? It is better for a man to be wise and learn from the word of God on how to manage the available resources in his possession because you have been destined to multiply. The wisdom on how to manage the resources that has been given to you by our God will be made manifest to you today by the grace of God.

III: Business

> *Whatsoever you do, do it with the whole of your heart as to the Lord and not man; for everything you do, your reward is in heaven. Colossians 3:23–34 KJV*

> *Seest thou a man diligent in his business He shall stand before kings; he shall not stand before mean men. Proverbs 22:29 KJV*

According to the above scripture, there are three strong words and these are as follows:

- Diligent
- Kings
- Mean men

Diligence is a characteristic whereby a man puts in consistency, efficiency, and goal-getting strategy in his or her business which ultimately transcends to less work and strategic achievement of set goals. When a man is diligent in his or her work or business, the Bible says this man will wine and dine with what is called the VIP of a particular organization or country basically because this individual's dedication to his work has caused the light of God to shine in his life which makes him a VIP. When a man is diligent in his or her work, it helps bring multiplication in his business which helps the business to grow, expand,

and gradually start operating a system of branch network. Listen, you cannot be poor when you are diligent in whatever you do especially in the area of business or profession you find yourself. The scripture has clearly stated it and God is not a man that He should lie.

Are you a businessman? What is the status of your business? I want you to know that one secret of a successful business is "diligence." When you started your business, were you diligent? And how has your business affected your life and those around you? Diligence helps your business multiply and also increase your status. It helps you meet your transactionary, precautionary, and speculative needs or activities of your business. When you are diligent, it catapults you to a greater height and places you on a top position in the industry where you operate.

A king is a ruler of an independent state, community, or country who hails from a royal family and has a particular domain under his jurisdiction with the responsibility to administer their daily inhabitation for the general good. He is the most important and influential person in the society where he lives, and his decisions affect the decision-making of the parliament in such a way that affects the generality of the population under his kingdom. In most cases, the decision of the king is final.

Mean men on the contrary are men that are not recognized in the area of affairs in the society. These are men that have very low life/self-esteem and in all ramification poor. These are men that have been eaten up by penury and are very poor in terms of self-actualization with no future, vision, and aspiration of life. They are referred to as men that exist but not living, and these men are not known for any memorable and outstanding achievement in life.

Diligence is a key that opens the door to any success in business. When a man is diligent, it helps this man strategize for the business growth; this is because all efforts are geared toward the growth of the investment. I am very sure you have heard many great men that have attained the greatest peak of what achievement is all about but have also gone down the drain of life. What you need to ask yourself is, why did these men go down the ladder? The simple answer is lack of persistence and diligence of attitude to work and also lack of the Holy Ghost in their business. You can only have good success by the help of God which is the spirit that helps you in all you do. You need to be persistent in all you do because this is the only reason for your success as you do not have any reason to be a failure. You have all it takes to make it in life; you are designed for a purpose and this purpose is to multiply in all you do for good.

It is either you succeed or fail in your life pursuit. The decision is yours to choose. There are no two ways around it; as Christians we are destined to be victorious in all we do. That is your destiny according to God's words, and the only condition is to be obedient to the word of God and keep His commandment. You might be wondering how to go about revitalizing your present state of business position, but I need to inform you that it is one very easy thing to do. All you have to do is meet quietly with our God in prayers and supplications in any form.

There are so many business seminars being organized by business experts on how your business(es) can grow in a world of competition from a global market perspective. Information is one of the keys to a successful business. A man who is not informed is deformed in the actual sense, and this is why you also need information in that area of business which can only come forth from a business expert in your field of business. Don't give up when things are down with you; all you need is a comprehensive dedication and diligence in your field of business because this is one of the keys to reaching for the sky. So many have tried it and it worked for them, and I am convinced in my spirit that if you do the same, the sky will be your stepping stone. Our God is hardworking and that is why He was able to create the heavens and the Earth in six days, and on the seventh day, He rested. Continue to put in your best if you have been doing that, and if you are becoming discouraged, I am boldly telling you now that you should go back with all effort to change the situation by putting together your resources in a clearly defined business then wait and see if God will not change things for the better. Are you trying to go into a particular business? What you need at this point in time is the Holy Spirit. Tell Him to guide you in the kind of business that you can invest your money in that will yield excellent result which will carry the glory of God in your life.

You need a well-prudent way to manage your finance at this moment for your future to be secured. God has given you the opportunity to explore the Earth because it is your inheritance. Don't be deceived; you are born to rule. All you just have to do is start having a great change of your mentality and hold on to your birthright by exercising the power of a royal inheritance. It is God's wish that you multiply in your finance. Come to think of it, is some of the resources that you earn from businesses or your annual income spent efficaciously to the glory of God? I want to believe you can see beyond the present. You need to inculcate into your habit the behavior or attitude of an ant.

> *Four things on earth are small, yet they are extremely wise: ants are creatures of little strength, yet they store up their food in the summer. Proverbs 30:24, 25 NIV*

You need to manage the little resources in your possession in an effective manner that would help you secure your future. It is quite a known fact to say that your resources are limited and your wants are unlimited. Now, how do you satisfy these unlimited wants? It is simply by judicious use of these limited resources. Critically looking at the attitude of an ant, they know quite alright that during winter, they cannot do anything because of the unfavorable harsh weather; they cannot go in search of anything but needs to secure their present and their future, and so, they work very hard during the summer and gather as much as they can during this season in order to stock up their store and also get what to depend on during an unbearable weather that is not friendly to their existence. How much more you that can withstand all situations by the Spirit of God that dwells inside of you? Do you know that ants do not have ears? But yet they are considered as one of the wisest animal on earth because of their remarkable nature of strategizing for the future.

> *It has no commander, no overseer or ruler, yet it stores its provisions in summer and gathers its food at harvest. Proverbs 6:7-8. NIV*

He who fails to plan plans to fail. Looking at the scripture above, you will discover that ants do not have any direct boss that controls nor tell them what to do. Rather, they are self motivated, focused and self controlling in their daily activities. God created a magnificent device and innate nature during an ant creative process that directs and teach he or she how to live successfully on earth. How much more you that is created in God's image and likeness with a process of creation that took some creative planning technique by the Almighty God. You need to plan for your finance and your future not mindful of any obstacle because it has been taken care of by your heavenly father. Surely they shall gather, but mind you they cannot succeed because they that are with you are more than they that are on the other side. The obvious fact that God has blessed you to multiply in your finance does not give you the opportunity to live a life without concrete planning for the unknown future which, of course, has been taken care of by your known God. You need to plan for your financial independence, and the only way you can do this is by seeking the face of God in the area of your finances.

A very good example in the scripture is Joseph. He was filled with the Spirit of God inside of him which transcended to making him the most knowledgeable and inspired person in Egypt. He interpreted dreams and had the understanding of the importance of an effectual saving habit in order to take care of the future by the revelation from the Most High God. One very important thing which he did was to hearken to the voice of God, and this singular obedience exposed him to a greater height that resulted to an opportunity of dining with the rulers of the ancient Egyptian kingdom. When famine took over the land, Egypt had plenty to eat because there was an accurate planning process which took place before the calamity visited the land, and during his office on the throne, Egypt never had a case of shortage of food. The land of Egypt became a major financial hub for those in need of money, food, and other material things for existence.

The money available at your disposal now is for a particular purpose; it is not by accident that God has put into your hands that little penny. If you remember the story of the three servants as narrated to us by our Lord Jesus Christ, you would understand what it means to be very proactive in our decisions concerning effective utilization of our resources. You need to start thinking in the right direction on how you will go about managing your limited funds. There are so many financial experts around you; all you need to do is to explore this opportunity and avail yourself of their services. You need to manage that money in your possession very well so that you will not regret or have this story of if I had known.

REPLENISH

And the Lord God took the man, and put him into the Garden of Eden to dress it and to keep it. Genesis 2:15 KJV

God's creation is perfect; and He saw that everything He created was good. He handed over the Earth to you in order for you to take very good care of it and to also replenish that which has been used by men in the process of co-inhabitation. The unfortunate aspect of this mandated process given to man is that man disappointed God in the Garden of Eden by going against His will and commandments.

Despite man's sinful nature, our Heavenly Father gave us the sole mandate to replenish the Earth, and it is one of our responsibilities ordained by God. The responsibility to perform this obligation and the ability to do this have been placed upon you when you were created. When He pronounced into your life to replenish, He meant that you should replace what has already been used by the Earth through the innate ability you have in your Spirit being. Having discovered this obvious fact, it is wise to say here that God has a particular responsibility that has been attached unto your life to be accomplished, and this you can do only by the help of His Spirit that quickens and activates your inner man. According to a careful study by researchers, during a fifty-year career of an average person on Earth, a minimum of 100,000 hours have been put into consistent nonstop work.

That He would grant you, according to the riches of his glory, to be strengthened with might by his Spirit in the inner man. Ephesians 3:16 KJV

Your physical and spiritual strength can only come from God. This is the more reason why you cannot do anything without the Holy Spirit. The question is how can one replenish the Earth? This is only by the Spirit of God in you who will activate the strength and power in you to be creative and help create an atmosphere that is filled with His glory and adoration through His anointing that has been bestowed upon you to do exploits for God.

There are so many times I walked either on the street or in a gathering where I get to see and meet people from different family backgrounds, traditions, and tribes. I always take note of something very important, and this is the diverse thinking mentality, belief, and attitude. Most times, after taking a close examination of these different backgrounds and how it affects the entire lives of these people, I discover that people have diverse and selfish interest towards one another.

God has designed human life in a perfect way by His wisdom and has a particular reason for doing this. When God created you and breathed into you through your nostril, He breathed into you wisdom, potential skills, talent(s), and power to replenish the Earth. God is a Spirit and cannot live on Earth; that is why He mandated you to take responsibility of all He has created and to always make sure it works in accordance to His laws of creation. According to the law of human creation, He created the Earth for only the ability of the of human, plants and other kinds of animals to survive in, and that was why Jesus had to come in the form of flesh through a virgin by the help of the Holy Ghost. If you do not carry out this mandate, there is no way the Earth can be replenished, and you are among those that have this special and unique potential to perform this rightful responsibility. God created you to replenish what He has already created because for every living thing on Earth, there is a life cycle assigned to it. It is only by the grace and power of God in our lives that we can effectively do that which has been spoken by God concerning our life through your inner man who can help you achieve this in your life.

I want to believe you are engaged in one activity of your choice either by free will or compulsion. To be honest with yourself, are you really in the right place where your potentials, skills, and talents are absolutely put into use for the manifestation of the glory of God in your life? Or you are just doing that which you find yourself doing out of compulsion in order to satisfy your needs or keep the body and soul together? What is your present state of mind of your quest in this world?

Taking a critical look at the African continent, would you personally say that the word of the Lord concerning replenishment has been fulfilled when compared to other developed countries? One problem with this continent is lack of the knowledge of God concerning the continent. This continent is blessed with abundance of human and natural resources, potentials, skills, power, and wisdom to replenish the continent, but she is going contrary to the word of God concerning the effective, efficient, and judicious utilization of the resources that are deposited in this continent for economic growth and prosperity. I am so convinced that the plan of God concerning this continent will be accomplished in the life of Africans by His grace and love for this part of the world. It is a continent filled with milk and honey.

Now, the question I would like to ask and expect you to answer is, looking at the developed countries and the African continent, what is the major reason for the high level of disparity in the level of growth and development between these two? The sooner the answer is known, the faster the solutions to the incessant breakdown and precarious state of the nation. I pray that God in His infinite mercies would help the African continent to start to put into active use the innate ability that He has deposited into this continent. On several occasions, I have taken time to take a close look at what is going on around me and the kind of people I meet. Anytime I am with some people, I see potentials and skills that can take them to places. But one major problem is lack of application of their potentials.

I have seen so many people work for so many years, and from a careful examination, close to half of the number of years they have spent in this world have been used to work for others, and at the end of the day, they would be relying on what they called gratuity and pension. This is one of the very mistakes our aged parents have made, and this same misconception is ravaging our present-day generation. They refuse to understand what God really wants for their lives, and they prefer to walk under the influence of their belief. Most people that I have been able to meet do not think of how they would one day become an employer, but rather how they would work for a particular company and earn an income for the rest of their life.

Anytime I listen to news on TV, and I happen to see pensioners knocking at the door of government, I usually have sympathy on these aged people. In our present world, so many pensioners have died in poverty with no care, medical attention, and financial obligation by the government. I have oftentimes heard some people say that "when I retire from the civil service, the Federal Government will pay my gratuity and pension." Most often, I feel so sorry for these people, and what surprises me the most is that it is these same government companies that have been privatized due to change in the recent government policy on indigenization policy. You don't put your trust in man or an institution but in God alone. You can become what God says you would be only if you start operating in the realm and come to the realization of this fact. I know you are born to rule and not to be ruled.

There is this very important thing I have noticed in the life of people in this present generation, and this is "Limitation by so-called paper or certificate." I know you would be astonished by this, but don't be; it is the truth and it has gone a long way in drawing so many people, organizations, and countries backward. I remember asking a group of people some questions on how they envision their future. Everyone have big dreams. The issue now is that, is it in reality based on your state of physical readiness? Maybe you have a dream and everything seems not to work well for you. In such case, then it might mean that probably you had a wrong dream which has refused to align with the potential in you for greater atmosphere of your existence.

When I was still in university, most of my classmates used to tell me that because they are studying a particular course, it meant that they would surely work in a big organization. One thing I noticed in their thoughts was nothing but lack of vision and foresight of what they were really made up of. Then I used to tell them of my vision, and they get so upset simply because they felt that it was too big and unachievable. I can vividly remember that some will just scream so loud and refused to understand that it is the spiritual manifestation that had giving me that confidence to stand on the true vision.

One thing that amazes me most about some people is that they prefer to work under someone to earn salary at the end of the month; it is alright, but they refuse to come to the realization that they too can employ someone to work for them. I refuse this philosophy of life that says some are born to rule and some are born to be ruled. This is against God's word. The scripture says that we all are equal before the heavenly throne. There is no way you can excel in a particular thing you do when you do not take pleasure and satisfaction in it. Success comes by first having a total commitment in whatever you do in a passionate manner. When you find something you do best and enjoy doing, don't hesitate to keep on doing it consistently. When you do this, you will be astonished with the level of your prosperity.

What part have you played in replenishing the Earth? Are you an engineer, a shoemaker, or fashion designer? Do you know that you have to play your own significant part to make this world a better place to live in? Success sometimes come by working hard and always trying to find pleasure in what you do; this is one way success can come. Please note that success is not measured only in monetary terms, but in achievements and contentment in other areas of your life. Where you are now and what you are doing are not by accident, and this you should know because you have a responsibility that is assigned to you by God to affect someone's life with whatever you find yourself doing. Whatever you do, always try to do it well as this will bring perfection which is the only criterion that will bring and attract people to your business, thereby helping your business grow.

I know someone who was once in charge of a business and did not manage the business properly. One day, I went to her to make some inquiries on why she does that to her boss. What she told me was amazing. She said that her boss does not trust her and does not even believe in anything that she does. As a result, she treats him that way by not helping his business grow. Her attitude usually scared customers away from coming to do more business with the company. After all the information gathered, I told her to take this job very seriously like she was the owner and to also see to the growth of the business. I also made her understand that this singular act could have a major implication on her personal life. This advice if yielded to can take her to a point in her life that her boss will build trust and entrust other things to her care. She never knew that when this business grows, the boss will not have any reason to doubt her capability. It was her level of commitment that had caused that level of lack of trust by her boss. Sometimes I would go there for her to render some services to me, but she will not be found in her office, and I was very sure that there were so many other people that have also come for the same reason and she would not be found to attend to them all because she intentionally wanted to punish her boss. She finally had a change of heart toward her job and resigned from the job after getting a better job somewhere else. But the most important thing was that she had a change of attitude and a better perspective to the things of life.

You need God's help to survive the unknown tomorrow. Why not commit your unknown tomorrow to the known God? You need to maximize the slightest opportunity that comes your way and explore the channel of blessing that had been apportioned to your life. At this point of your life, you need to build for yourself a level of trust in God that can cause changes in all aspects of your life. The word has been spoken to you, and the word of God does not go void not until it accomplishes that which had been said. You do not have any choice over this issue. You must replenish the Earth as you know that is one of your responsibilities in life. What you need now is to critically examine your life and carry out an extensive research of how you can start exploring the opportunities that have been given unto you and start acting like someone who is created to replenish the Earth through some innate abilities you have inside you.

> *And every skillful person in whom the lord has put skill and understanding to know how to perform all the work. Exodus 36:1 KJV*

Our God who placed a great responsibility on you to take care of His Earth also took upon Himself the responsibility of ensuring the skills and knowledge to replenish the Earth were bestowed on you. When you look at the process of human civilization and its origin, you will discover the ancient civilization originated from Africa (Egypt). Our God is omniscient; He knows the end from the beginning, and that is why He placed on man that innate ability to invent and discover and created what man will need for a peaceful and successful coexistence and replenishment of the Earth.

SUBDUE

> *And the seventy returned again with joy, saying, Lord, even the devils are subject unto us through thy name. And He said unto them, I beheld Satan as lightning fall from heaven. Behold, I give you power to tread on serpents and scorpions, and over all the power of the enemy: and nothing shall by any means hurt you. Luke 10:17–19 KJV*

Why are you still in that precarious situation despite your inheritance in Christ Jesus? I need you to understand that you have been given the power to rule over every creature either living or dead on planet Earth. Listen, do not be deceived there is something inside of you that has not been explored. Immediately when you were born, your first breath signified a significant threat in the camp of the enemy because you are a child of God who has come to fulfill God's word on Earth; that is why the process of your formulation in your mother's belly cannot be explained, according to the scripture which says that "even before you were formed in the belly, I knew you" this is our God speaking. You are special and have a mission on Earth. Please know this: you are not on Earth just to fill up some space. Every single creature created by God has a purpose and mission to fulfill; it is left for you to discover and identify your purpose on Earth.

Situations of life have got so many people especially Christians to fall short of God's plan for their lives. I get so astonished when I hear that life's situation has got some folks down and at the same time these set of people proclaim they are serving our living God who knows the problems and worries of His people. He is always ready to turn their life situation around if only they will accept and start to work in line with the creator's rules and commandments. Do you know that this can only be done by their understanding of His words for their lives? The surprising issue here is that these set of people have forgotten that it had been spoken into their lives to subdue the Earth, and this can only come to manifestation by the level of the knowledge of God's word upon their lives which can only work by the inner man inside of you.

To subdue means to put under control situations around or confronting you to work in your favor and according to your wish either by force or other means. You can subdue by your words or action. In your tongue lies power. There is power in the tongue which is one of the weapons that can be used to subdue an unpleasant situation that comes your way. You can also subdue by your actions, by acting in accordance to what you believe in. Take, for instance, when troops are ordered to forcefully put under control rebels terrorizing a particular domain or area. We all have witness of this in our present global leadership trends concerning a particular motive either of political, economic, or social interest. The most important fact about subdue is to protect an individual or nation's interest against his or her opponent that is not in support of what has been originally planned for.

You cannot be weighed down by life's circumstances. Whenever I hear such words, I get disappointed and see these people as spiritually illiterate not because they are dull but because they lack knowledge of the understanding of God's words. God has built in their inner man the ability to withstand any discouraging life situation. Get this straight, life's situation can't weigh you down; you have power over any situation that comes your way and only you can take charge and also determine how you want it to be. The truth of the matter is that you should be the one who is the major determinant of your life and not circumstances acting as determining factors of your life.

There are circumstances that you face which helps to determine your faith in God. The story of Job who was faced with an unpalatable life circumstance that was beyond human understanding was a typical example. It was the revelation through God's word that made him put all his trust in God. He trusted God for breakthrough because he knew it was only temporal. One thing I notice in so many people is that life circumstance brings them closer to God, and this is not supposed to be like that. If you are one of such, you need forgiveness because such people will keep living a life filled with troubles not until they genuinely come to God with a sincere heart to serve Him and not for a selfish motive. Job had a brighter and well-structured future because at the end he also believed God as a result of the faith he exercised during his trial period.

Some time ago, I was discussing with a friend on a cool evening and we started talking about life and its inhabitants coupled with God's creation. Then suddenly, I heard her say that it is not every one that is meant to be wealthy in life for some are meant to be poor and others to be rich. Immediately, I rebuked her! I told her to reverse those words and that it is not true. She insisted that it is the truth. What I told her was, "show me from the scripture where God said to some people go into the world and remain poor." She had forgotten that God's wish for us all is to prosper and his thought toward us is not of evil but good and sound mind to bring us to our expected end.

I made her understand that her thought is man's philosophy and from the bottomless pit of hell. How can a man live in Christ the hope of glory, and still continue to live in penury? Poverty is a sin and it is a sin to live a life with poverty. Listen, you can't be poor but will only be if you choose to be poor. There are some believers that have eaten up and betrayed God's divine purpose for their lives and not until this fact is put into the right place of what He really wants from us, things might continue to be difficult for some folks. You have everything you need at your disposal. What you need is right in front of you. Grab and possess it, God has created you for good and He has blessed you in all ramifications of life. By this singular reason, the idea of penury is erased from your life. Failure is only in the dictionary of the foolish, and this you can overcome by the level of your knowledge in God's word and plan for your life.

> *And from the days of John the Baptist until now the kingdom of God suffereth violence, and the violent take it by force. Matthew 11:12 KJV*

I have a very close friend who is full with God's word and knows the importance of being a blessing to people around her. On one hot afternoon, I saw her with some security agents in an unpleasant situation, and then I drew closer. On getting there, I was astonished with what I saw. I had to meet with the security men in a more peaceful manner and other people intervened to reduce the level of argument and to also create an atmosphere of peace. Later that day, I went to her and told her that I was surprised to have seen her involved in that violent situation, and her reply was that nobody can take her for granted or step on her right. She also told me that she knows the law and live by the law; no one can tramp on her rights. She now explained everything to me and I understood the reasons for her actions. As a Christian, we need to work in accordance to the laws where we inhabit and keep to the rules and regulations of our leaders.

Being a Christian does not mean you should not know your right and abide by the rules and regulations governing the environment you find yourself. Knowing your right and protecting your right does not mean disobeying the rules and regulations of the state. Some Christians would say "I am meek," and yes that is true. One of the gifts of the Holy Spirit is meekness, but that does not mean you should not know your right. Jesus Christ knew His right and abided by the rules and regulations of the land while He was on Earth for His mission and purpose. But He never allowed His right to be taken from Him. He said to give to Caesar what is Caesar's and to God what is of God which goes a long way to explain the importance of protecting and respecting an individual's rights and also abiding by the laws of the land.

Have you ever been faced with situations that made you feel bad? There are some situations you have to take charge of. One way is through force; the only language the devil understands is the language full with authority. You have to stand your ground for what you really want and how you want it done. Do not be satisfied with your present state of mind if you are still operating below God's divine purpose for creating you. Are you facing a situation that seems impossible to provide solution by men? But to Christ, it is one of the easiest issues in your life. You might be out there with one sickness or the other; all you need is the word of God concerning your health. To the best of my knowledge,

Jesus Christ on the cross took away all manners of sickness and not some manners of sickness, so the only way sickness can weigh you down is if Jesus Christ had left some sicknesses which He did not. Rather He took away all our infirmities for He is the God that healeth thee.

He is the God that can make a way in the desert and river in the wilderness which invariably means that your life cannot be a life full of dryness and lack. No matter the situation you are currently facing right now, all you need is to exercise God's word in your life, speak the word, exercise the word, apply the word, and start manifesting a life that you deserve to live. You have a life to live that cannot be compared with that of the world and this is the life that Christ has given unto you, and always remember that you have power over everything that comes your way by His grace and power in your life.

I know a man who got a job from one of the topmost multinational organizations by force; don't be surprised by the word "force" because of what happened. He had no connection in the company but forced himself into one of the top positions from the street. I am very sure you would want to know how he did it. What he did was to go into the company's premises and told the receptionist that he wanted to see the human resource manager. He was asked by the receptionist if he had an appointment; he replied that the personnel manager will be glad to have him in his office. He was allowed to see him. When he got to his office, they exchanged pleasantries after which he told him that he needed a job in the company because he had been jobless for some years, and the manager replied, "I am sorry, we don't have space for you at the moment." The next day he went again and requested to see the manager saying he had an appointment with him and was once again allowed in. But this time on a different appearance, getting to the manager's office, the manager said, "I guess you were here yesterday looking for a job and I told you there was none presently for you?" Then he replied again, "Have you got a space for me now? It is about the twenty fourth hour that the manager replied, "no space for you at the moment."

He continued this exercise the third day, and the manager became furious, sent him away never to return, and ordered the receptionist not allow to allow him to his office anymore. On the fourth day, he disguised himself and returned again. Then on the fifth and last faithful day, he was told to drop his resume. During the same period, an advertisement was placed and this young man's resume was an exact match with the advertised position. He was interviewed, passed and was called to resume immediately, and his employment letter was handed over to him.

If we take a close look at this man's life, you will discover that he took complete charge of his destiny and future and totally refused to live a life that is below God's plan for him. Any position you find yourself is a function of your understanding of God's word. The life you live now is all about choice, and you can decide to change your life for the better and also decide to remain in that position if you decide to. What I am trying to say is that you have the power to change your life's situation. Don't be deceived; God will not come down from heaven to do that for you. You have a personal responsibility to change your situation for good because he has given you the power to positively transform your life to the glory of His name. The power to cause things to work in your favor has been given unto you.

No matter the situation you are facing, it might not be a situation of joblessness but one particular thing that you are believing God for and things seems to be discouraging, don't give up but hold on to your dream for the vision is for an appointed time. He is not asleep, nor His ears too heavy to hear your worries. He has a plan for you which of course is to subdue and make situations bow to you. The very day you start exhibiting fear about life's situations, it marks the day you start deviating from God's plan for your life. You need to be bold like a lion and keep saying the word everyday as long as you live because this will activate your inner man by his Spirit that dwells in you which would culminate into the manifestation of His purpose for you. Knowing fully well that the words we speak are very important and have a long way in influencing our lives and entire future, so start exercising the power you have by the authority that we have in Christ to start speaking to that financial, spiritual, and physical difficulty to flee from your life because you bear on you the mark of Christ. There is no way you can please God without faith for it is a mechanism or channel that bridges the gap between you and God. When you speak words backed by faith in Christ, you tend to bring down God's glory upon your life which helps bring down His blessing.

All I have to tell you is to live a life that has control over your situation for it is your inheritance and blessing that has been placed upon you which is a privilege. It is a word that has been spoken to your inner man, and as long as you live, that word will continue to radiate and live in you. But in so many people's lives, such words are inactive, ineffective, and dormant, as such people refuse to operate under the influence of the Holy Spirit which has led to their misfortune and lack of vision. They have refused the Comforter to take charge of their lives. I am so convinced that you can make it, but you cannot become that which God wants you to be without the help of the Holy Spirit. All you need is to develop your inner man and start seeing yourself as someone who is very important and you cannot be overshadowed by life circumstances.

DOMINION

Dominion is a state of absolute control of a particular situation. God during human creation created man to be in charge of His divine creation. There is no way God's chosen children would be under subjection and control by the adversaries. It amazes me when I see people live a life of fear. People always have this notion of a life dominated with the adversaries, and the moment you start living such life, the devil will start to capitalize on this to instill fear in you, and when you start living a life of fear, your spirit will be far away from the heavenly throne.

A spoken word of God cannot go void until it accomplishes what has been assigned to it. You have some primary responsibilities on Earth, and if these responsibilities are not perfectly achieved, you will be held liable. A word has been spoken upon your life from the heavenly throne. When God said unto your life, "dominate," He meant take charge of the world, go and posses the Earth, and live a life that is worth living in His sight. You have everything you need at your disposal only if you start tapping from your God-given treasure. God has given unto you all you need in life to help you carry on with trial and precarious situations around you. His favor is upon you to break through life's circumstances because Christ on the cross has already broken through on your behalf. He has placed upon you His wisdom and blessings which are above every other thing on Earth.

There are some times when I look at some people's lives and compare it with the word of God; what I always discover is a very high percentage of distinction or variance between the word of God and a perfect way of life. So many are contented with the position they find themselves, and it is very wrong for it is contrary to the will of God for their lives, and this grieves God because He has placed in everyone potentials of gifts to excel. There are blessings packaged for us by God, and all you need do is to decree your birthright. It is your right to have a very good and conducive environment of life that is filled with the blessings of God which brings abundance and adds no sorrow. When a man has dominion, he operates under the following:

Abundance

> *And the Lord shall make thee plenteous in goods, in the fruit of thy body, and in the fruit of thy cattle, and in the fruit of thy ground, in the land which the Lord sware unto thy fathers to give thee. The Lord shall open unto thee his good treasure, the heaven to give the ram unto thy land in his season and to bless all the work of thine hand; and thou shalt lend unto many nations, and thou shalt not borrow. Deuteronomy 28:11–12 KJV*

Do you know that you can never lack? Okay, let's put it this way, for clarity's sake, do you know you must not borrow? Alright, maybe you have not yet gotten what I am trying to pass across. Do you know God has sworn unto your life to be fruitful? Maybe you will get it now; do you know you are blessed to be a blessing to nations? Thus says the Lord.

Not until you come to the realization of these facts, you will not be operating in the divine realm which you are supposed to be operating. You are not supposed to be operating at a low level of lack, of penury, and a miserable life filled with financial crisis. You cannot lack; this is because it is a fact. The scripture says that you will never lack for you will have plenty and will be fruitful in your soul and body. He will open unto you treasures and nations will come unto you for blessings.

You need God's own type of mentality to live in this wicked world we live in, for we are not of this world but we live in this world. Do you know that you are from Zion? A Zionite can never and will never lack; they are blessings to nations and the good of the land shall never cease from their household because as a Zionite, there is a special interest of the celestial being on such people.

I used to have a friend when I was in school and he is still my good friend; so many people find it so hard to know the actual state he is from because anytime he was asked, "where are you from?" His answer was always Zion and this answer gets some of these people angry to the extent that they get infuriated. You cannot beg for food; It is the fact. Things might be a little bit contrary but it will not last long; this is because the end justifies the means. The economic situation of the country and the world at large cannot determine your future for your future is in the hand of the Almighty God.

When God said unto your life, "be fruitful," He meant you should go and possess the Earth and live a life that is worth living in His sight. You have everything at your disposal only if you start tapping from God's given treasure which has been made to bless you. God has given unto you all you need in life to help you carry on. His favor is upon you to break through life circumstances; this is because Christ on the cross has already broken through on your behalf. Life circumstances cannot weigh you down because Christ on the cross has automatically made you a favored and chosen one of God. He has placed upon you His wisdom and blessings which are above every other thing on Earth.

Sometimes, when I study some people and compare it with the word of God, what I always notice is a very high percentage of distinction or variance between these two judgmental parameters. So many are contented with the position they find themselves and it is very wrong. It is contrary to the will of God for such lives, and this grieves the Almighty God because He has placed in everyone some potentials and gift to excel in life and wisdom to physically and spiritually transform your life situation. There are blessings packaged for us by God, but He needs you to tap into this hidden treasure and exercise your birthright. It is your right to be in a very pleasant and conducive environment of life that is filled with the blessings of God which brings abundance and adds no sorrow.

Start seeing yourself as a giver and a blessing to nations because that is who you are and it is your birthright; all you have to do is change your mentality and start working in the environment where you are destined to operate. You are born to affect those lives around you in a positive way, and that is why you are in that particular place at this moment for a particular reason. That same person who needs your help is waiting for you to reach out to his or her situation. I know you are now a changed person on Earth. There are two very important things that you have to do in order to start operating in that right realm which you are supposed to operate are: first and foremost, to have the right attitude and to love your neighbors as you love yourself. It is a medium and channel to give with your whole heart and that is what God recognizes.

> *And he increased his people greatly; and made them stronger than their enemies. Psalm 105:24 KJV*

Developing a right attitude and a lovely heart to rendering help brings down God's favor upon your life. It creates a way for you where there seems to be no way and rivers in the desert. A right attitude toward giving apprehends God's blessings into your life. Having a good attitude toward giving helps you achieve God's divine purpose for your life. All you need is to be diligent in all you do and put your trust in Him and Him alone for your future endeavors.

Remember that a child's foolishness is bound in his heart but a rod of correction takes this child from such foolish behavior. Any man that oppresses the poor to enrich himself shall end up with a miserable life, and you that giveth the little you have to an unproductive activity shall surely come to want for such will not help increase the little he has which reduces the level and honor of such man on the face of the Earth. A word is enough for the wise and you cannot do without having a godly heart toward your neighbors in need.

CHAPTER FIVE

THE PRINCIPLE OF GIVING

There is one vital principle of life that would help you operate in that very position God wants you to operate in life; and this is a principle called "giving." There are some significant spiritual connection between a man with an attitude of willful giving and his rewards in heaven and on Earth. The Bible says, "It is more blessed to be a giver than a receiver." When you are a giver, you are forcefully opening the windows of heaven for blessings into your life.

> *Blessed is he that considereth the poor: the Lord will deliver him in time of trouble. The Lord will preserve him, and keep him alive; and he shall be blessed upon the earth: and thou wilt not deliver him unto the will of his enemies. The Lord will strengthen him upon the bed of languishing: thou wilt make all his bed in his sickness. Psalm 41:1–3 KJV*

Have you for once considered giving a lending hand, helping, or being a blessing to those around you? You are always in contact with individuals that are in perpetual or abject poverty. Get it very clear, when we say give, it does not only apply to monetary giving; it could be other resources such as time, commitment, advice, and so on. When you depart unto eternal glory, you will be made accountable for all you have done. Our Lord Jesus Christ said, "When I was hungry, did you feed me? When I was naked, did you clothe me? When I was sick, did you visit me? When I needed your help, were you there for me? In times of trouble just as the Lord delivered you, were you committed to helping me?" All these questions you will be made to answer. But if you keep His words on these principles, He will preserve you in times of trouble and make your enemies bow down to you. Giving transcends beyond financial commitment, as previously said. It is all physically and spiritually encompassing. You can give your time, skills, and commitment to the things of the spirit and humanity for the world to be a better place. When you give, you are tapping directly into God's given purpose on Earth because your life and your future will never lack.

Having carried out a study of the benefits of giving, I came to the realization that those that give enjoy the good fruit of the land. Take, for example, the disparity between the advanced or developed and the developing country. You will notice that they are prospering because of one basic principle and this is giving. They do not lack, although they have needs, so does this apply to an individual. When you cultivate the habit of giving, both the spiritual and physical forces will be working in your favor because there are so many people depending on you to liberate them from their situations, likewise when compared to the developed countries that are advancing in all spheres of life. When you give, it is one way of singing praise and obeying God's commandment.

Moreover, looking at these countries, they give grants and aids to many poor countries, but unknown to these poor countries, they have been used as a channel to tap into God's blessing upon their land, and that is why you see these countries give every time and the developing nations at the receiving end. As the years go by, these developing nations accumulate huge debts upon their land leading to impoverishment of the citizens of the country. It is a principle that has been proven over time, and this principle can only work for those who apply it into their personal lives because of its importance. Learn to be a giver and not a receiver. To be a giver is not dependent on your status in life. You have some people around you that are in need; all you need to do is become a blessing to them with anything you can, and it could be financial and/or moral assistance.

> *Give and it shall be given unto you; good measure pressed down, and shaken together, and running over, shall men give into your bosom. For with the same measure that ye mete withal it shall be measured to you again. Luke 6:38 KJV*

The benefit you tend to reap from the attitude of giving is enormous. When you give, you will definitely receive the reward from heaven and on Earth. When you cultivate the act of giving, it helps you live a better life that is exceedingly greater than your imagination. When you give, your expectation would be exceedingly great because you have been given the opportunity to tap into a divine principle of life that can help you live a life that God has programmed.

"Start seeing yourself as a giver and a blessing to nations because that is who you are"; all you have to do is change your mentality and start working in the atmosphere where you are destined to operate. You are born to positively impact those around you, and that is why you are in that particular place for a particular reason. I believe that with God, you are now a changed person on Earth. One very important thing is that you have to give with the right attitude and love. Giving with the right attitude and a pure heart is what God recognizes, and it will help catapult you to your assigned purpose because you will increase in all spheres of life.

> *And he increased his people greatly; and made them stronger than their enemies. Psalm 105:24 KJV*

As I rightly said, developing an excellent attitude and a lovely heart to giving helps bring down God's favor upon your life. It creates a way for you where there seems to be no way and makes a river in the desert. A right attitude toward giving apprehends God's blessings into your life. You need to have a good attitude toward giving. All you need is to be diligent in all you do and put your trust in Him and Him alone for your future plans.

Remember that a child's foolishness is bound in his heart, but a rod of correction takes this child farther from such foolish behavior. Any man that oppresses the poor to enrich himself shall end up with a miserable life and you that giveth the little you have to unproductive activities shall surely come to want for such will not help increase the little he has which reduces the level and honor of such a man on the face of the Earth. A word is enough for the wise for you cannot do without having a godly heart toward your neighbors in need.

CHAPTER SIX

HINDRANCES TO GOD'S PURPOSE FOR YOUR LIFE

There are several ways you can hinder God's purpose for your life, and they are indirectly proportional or dependent on the tenacity and dexterity of your spiritual man's love for the works of the heavenly race. There are so many scriptural references of so many men and women who lost God's plans for their lives. Some of the ways you can hinder the purpose of God for your life are as follows:

- Sin
- Putting your trust in man

- Worldly association
- Unfaithfulness
- Disobedience

SIN

Whenever we sin, it means we have consciously or unconsciously missed the mark of God's standard for our lives as Christians. Our Lord Jesus Christ came to this world and paid the price for the consequence of our sins. When a human consciously engages in any evil act it means that the connecting cord between God and such a man has been destroyed. Sin is a premeditated and deliberate act by any human to go against God's commandment. When God created the heavens and earth, God had a plan for humans to live a blissful life on earth with all creatures through His divine purpose for creating man, but by one man (Adam) sin entered the world with a consequence of everlasting death. For all have sinned and come short of the glory of God, but our Lord Jesus Christ came to give us everlasting life through grace. When a man sins, he spiritually distances himself from God. Sin is a state of bondage and danger to any soul on Earth. If you read through the scripture, you will discover that the consequences of sin in the life of God's chosen generations are so devastating that you begin to wonder that despite the knowledge so many Christians have about living a life of sin, some Christians still indulge in the act of unrighteousness.

Imagine when a person is tied up with a heavy stone and thrown into an ocean. He or she without contention will gravitate in accordance to the weight down into the bottom of the ocean, that is how it is when a man is tied up in sin. Sin hinders a lot of good things to come to manifestation in a man's life, and that is why it is very pertinent to live a life free of sin and to also endeavor to reconcile our old ways with our Lord. Please, I plead with you and for the purpose of your eternal life to live a life that is free of sin. You can do it by the grace and power of God upon you.

Do not be deceived, there are consequences for going against God's divine principle. The scripture made us to understand and know that the wages of sin is death which of course does not translate to a physical death but goes beyond a transitory process of a human soul leaving its physical body. The reward for sin encapsulates both physical and spiritual death that is everlasting. When we say the output of going astray in the heavenly definition of sin, it means missing every single heavenly benefits for the chosen generation. God still loves you and He is ready to work with you for your purpose to be made manifest on Earth. Do not worry about your past; God still needs you in His kingdom. In the same ratification, there is no human on earth that is without sin, in sin is a human conceived, but we have eternal life through Jesus Christ our Lord who has come to redeem humans to our heavenly Father.

There are so many people that continually indulge themselves in unrighteous activities and are very comfortable in such acts with a consolation that our God is forgiving in nature. Be not deceived, the devil has set a very dangerous trap that has led so many to hell. Whatsoever a man sow, that will he reap. Do not allow the devil manipulate you into surrendering your purpose for things that are temporal. You have the spirit of God in you that will teach, guide and direct you on the right things to do.

I have seen and heard people say that they are struggling with an addiction because of their past relationship with someone or a group of people. It is a fundamental fact to say that the kind of association a man finds himself has a consequential impact on the nature of his or her lifestyle. Do not be deceived, the only way you can win an unhealthy lifestyle is to stay away from a particular set of people. You might not know it; the friends you keep have a way of influencing your behavior. If you have friends that are involved in ungodly acts, in no time, you will also be involved in such activities except if you consciously stay away and cut yourself off from such association.

When you pray to God with a heart filled with hatred and all manners of sins, do you think God will answer your prayers. The prayer of a sinner is an abomination in the sight of God. This is because, the iniquity of a sinner has separated him or her from God and when this happens, God will definitely not be in the affairs of such a man because His face has been hidden from him and whatever prayer of such a soul to God, it will not get to the sky. That is why there are so many unanswered prayers which is as a result of the intense sinful nature of men.

Sodom and Gomorrah is a biblical example of the consequence of engaging in sin and ungodly acts. The men and women according to the scripture were involved in all manners of sin such as fornication, adultery, murder, drunkenness and so many inexplicable acts that is against God's divine plan for man. According to the scripture, there was not even a single soul that was Christ-like, as a result of this, the city was destroyed and eliminated from the face of the earth. When I look at the current trends on earth and this generation, I discovered that it is exactly a replication of what happened in Sodom and Gomorrah which led to her destruction. The devil will always make sinners see their ways right but the output of such life is destruction.

In every country there are laws and principles that are expected of everyone to abide by and if anyone go against these sets of principles or laws, it is counted as transgression against the law. When a man sins against God, it is counted as transgression against the heavenly principles and laws with a consequence which is everlasting death in the pit of hell. Any man that sins against God shall surely die. On judgement day, every man shall bear the consequence of his or her action. A man's progenies will not bear the iniquities of his parents. The righteousness of a man will be counted for him alone so shall the wicked nature of some people. The only reason why generations suffer from the consequences of their parents is when God places a curse on a man and his generations through an act of transgressions against the laws of God.

Do you know that God did not spare Lucifer and his angels that rebelled against the host of heavens? So shall He not spare sinners that have deliberately gone against His laws and commandments on earth. Every soul that sins, shall be preserved for everlasting judgment which shall be upon those that transgress against God's laws on earth. There is good news, if a sinner confesses his or her sins with all sincerity and a heavy heart, our God is faithful and just to forgive such sins and also cleanse such soul from all unrighteousness.

PUTTING YOUR TRUST IN MAN

Once upon a time, a father set forth on a journey with his son to a village and told him to put all his trust in him alone and never to trust anyone. On getting to a village, he told his son to call on him anytime he needs anything that will make him happy. One day, the village was invaded by some stalkers, during this time, the boy looked to his right and left but could not find his father who was supposed to protect him because everyone was seeking protection from the invaders. This same young man obviously knew that his father ran and left him to scale through such a precarious situation without rendering any help to him. In order words, his father told him that he is just obeying the first law of human preservation which means every man for himself. After this terrifying experience, his father told him that he took such a deliberate act because, in life it is every man for himself. Another day, his father told him to go the roof of his house and told him to jump down, so he obeyed and climbed to the top of the house. As he was about to jump down, his father told him that he was going to catch him and not allow him to injure himself, as he jump down, his father drifted away from the direction he was and placed a bouncing object that will protect him from injuring himself. The young man then asked his father Why he deceived him? His father's response was: trust no man on earth, not even yourself, but God alone.

The Bible says woe unto a man who put his trust in men. You can only trust a human being and not human nature. Human beings have a natural tendency to disappoint you. Imagine putting your trust in someone that has the tendency to disappoint you; it is a very devastating and precarious situation that needs God's intervention. I have heard instances where people betrayed close friends, siblings, and relationships. I cannot imagine putting my trust in man who has the tendency to disappoint me. Any man who puts his trust in his fellow man has failed from the beginning.

I have seen and heard of people betrayed by their loved ones and so many have experienced hard times simply because of their inability to yield to God's word of not putting their trust in man. Never make the mistake of trusting a man; the moment you put your trust in man, this means that this person has taken a significant portion of your life. When you put your trust in a man, it means you no longer operate under the influence of the direction and instruction of the Holy Spirit in your life. There is a difference between putting your trust in the things of this world and the things of Heaven's throne. Putting your trust in the Heavenly throne is the only avenue to reach your full potentials. When you put your trust in God alone, He would specially take care of your needs. Putting your trust in God will cause Him to elevate you in all ways. I admonish you to stop putting your trust in man but in God alone for your eternal salvation.

You can only put your trust in God and not a man. When you put your trust in God through faith, it is counted as righteousness. Any man that puts his or her trust in man has been programmed to fail from the beginning. How can a man put his trust in a mortal being that has the potential of disappointing him? Please do not place your trust in anyone. Every human on earth has a secret and it is not advisable for anyone to share his or her secrets with anyone because, your perceived best friend today can be your enemy tomorrow and definitely, this person can use this secrets against you. Keep the secret of your inner man to yourself.

The bible said, curse be the man that put his trust in his fellow man. When a man put his trust in man and not God, it is counted as unrighteousness in the sight of God because his heart has departed from God who is the author and finisher of his faith. You do not owe any man trust but love which supersedes all things to help a man fulfill the laws of God through abiding by His commandments. One of the vital ingredients for your salvation as a Christian is your faith which is in Jesus through the gift of God. In as much you cannot deny the fact that you have to be at peace with all men, this does not mean that you should put your trust in men. The innate manifestation of human nature will definitely disappoint you, but God cannot deny you in time of need. There is nothing impossible for you to do through Jesus Christ which is in you. Christ in you, is the hope of glory, power and blessings which strengthens your inner man. When you put your trust in God alone, he will put songs of praise in your mouth and disappoint your enemies.

Cursed is the man that puts his trust in mere mortal for the end thereof will not be in accordance to his expectations. Some may put their trust in Horses and some in chariot, but we Christians will always put our trust in our God. Seek ye first the kingdom of God and His righteousness and everything you need both on earth and after you depart shall be added to you. When you put your trust in God, He will prepare a table before you in the presence of your enemies with a cup running over, pressed down shaken together. I must tell you that there are enormous benefits of putting your trust in the Lord which is your hope of salvation. Our God is a jealous God which means that he will not be happy with you if you reference another god or put your trust in men. He wants the best for you and that is why you must trust in Him alone for a better future.

WORLDLY ASSOCIATION

Do not be deceived: "Bad company corrupts good morals."
1 Corinthians 15:33 NASB

Recently, I carried out a study of how so many Christians have been indulged in worldly activities. It came to my notice that clubs and bars usually have high sales volume on weekends especially on Sundays. I sometimes ask myself that is it that so many people go to church just for the purpose of fulfilling all righteousness and not forsaking the assembling of the brethren? Going to church does not mean salvation is assured, and the most amazing fact is what happens sometimes among Christians even in the church. It takes the power and spirit of God to lead and direct us as Christians in the path of righteousness through Christ.

As Christians, we are not supposed to indulge in worldly association because there are no benefits in such activities. Visiting clubs, bars, and other places attracts evil atmosphere and does not in any way attract the spirit of God in our lives as Christians. It is very important that we separate ourselves from worldly association in order to live a life that is filled with the power of God. One way of separating ourselves from God as Christians is to be involved in worldly associations which does not glorify God on Earth. When you are involved in worldly association, it means that you have been separated from our heavenly Father. In such an instance, your name has automatically been erased from the book of life because your inner man has been polluted and you have distanced yourself from the kingdom of God.

When you are involved in worldly association, it means you have joined the masses in their evil ways. One very negative impact and consequences of associating yourself in worldly association is your inability to discern the things of the spirit because your inner man has been polluted and God is no longer in charge of the affairs of such a person which of course will give room for the enemies to penetrate and cause harm in such life. I have seen where a man filled with the anointing of the Holy Spirit turn away from the things of God through worldly association. It might not be an intentional decision, but through the negative influence of such association. Your friends and the kind of relationships you keep speaks loud to show who you are. If you associate yourself with those that find delight in committing sin, there is no way you will not be influenced into committing sin. As a Christian, you can identify sinners and ensure you convert them into the kingdom of God. This does not mean that you will constantly indulge yourself in their ungodly activities. Your lifestyle should be worth emulating. You must have a positive impact in the lives of those around you for a better society and for the salvation of their souls. The heart of a man is desperately wicked. When you are associated with a group of people that are not in Christ, you are bound to all manners of evils, wickedness and iniquity because such association gives birth to a life filled with misery.

An example is Daniel, according to the scripture, despite the fact that he was a highly respected man from a princely lineage, he decided in his heart that he will not partake of the king's meat. Rather, he kept his faith and trust in the Lord and constantly prayed and offered a holy sacrifice unto God. This made God open his kingdom and His blessings upon him. His life revealed and showed God in display in all ramification. He constantly preached the word of God to the kings he served during his time and constantly stood by the truth no matter the circumstances and situations he was faced with. He held on to God and put all his trust in the Lord and did not follow the traditions of men but kept his faith in God. His life revealed God in all areas even when there was a plot by his enemies to set him up negatively in the presence of king Darius through a decree which stated that all prayers should be directed to only the king and no other gods for thirty days. But Daniel decided in his heart that he will serve only our heavenly father and prayed only to the Lord God almighty. He was thrown into the Lions den but God and the host of angels were with him to the amazement of his enemies.

Let the light shine so bright that people will see God in your life. It does not matter who you are and where you are right now, you can always have a positive influence on those around you. Avoid all manners of worldly associations that will not glorify God in your life and do not walk in the counsel of the ungodly and wicked who take pleasure in committing sins. There is a plague awaiting sinners, adulterers, fornicators and those engaged in worldly associations that does not glorify God on earth.

UNFAITHFULNESS TO GOD

From the existence and history of humans on Earth, there have been several cases and consequences of living a destructive life as a result of unfaithfulness in the affairs of our Heavenly Father. God in His infinite mercy has given us commandments and principles of life in order for us to live perfect lives according to His principles. There is no way you can experience the gift of salvation if you are not faithful to God.

Unfaithfulness in whatever form either spiritually or physically to God is a destructive path that is lined up and ready for a future of doom. It is very important we stand faithful and steadfast to the laws and commandments of God. Unfaithfulness to God does not only apply to Christians, it also applies to nations. There are several nations that have long been very far away from God through their unfaithfulness. A critical look at some economic indices and indicators, you will realize that God is not in the affairs of such nations and the consequence of this is a destructive ending. It is very unfortunate to see that so many people and nations are still unfaithful to God and the consequences are inexplicable. When a man is unfaithful in the affairs of God on earth, there is no way such a man can expect to receive blessings from the heavenly kingdom. Unfaithfulness is a great sin which has hindered so many individuals and nations from achieving their potentials. Unfaithfulness to God breeds eternal destruction because, anyone found not faithful to the affairs of the kingdom of God has invited unto his own presence demons and satanic influence which obviously gravitate him or her towards the wide road. God counts our faith in Him as righteousness, so also our unfaithfulness as a sin. Have you wondered why so many people experience poverty and lack, it is because they are unfaithful to God. God is not a man that He should lie, let's get it straight, when a man is not faithful to God, he or she cannot experience everlasting peace, joy, prosperity and victory.

Scripturally, there are several instances where God tested the faith of some men in Him. An example is Abraham who was faithful to God. God counted his faith as righteousness. His name was changed from Abram to Abraham which means, the father of all nations. God tested his faithfulness when Abraham was instructed to sacrifice his only son Isaac on Moriah, through faith and trust in the most-high God, He obeyed God and offered him as a sacrificial lamb unto God. But God saw that he was faithful and instructed that he should not but offer him a ram instead of his son. A critical lesson from the story is that, God knows our challenges and also what we are passing through, but sometimes he wants to know if we are faithful at all times whether good or bad. I have heard and seen some people say they will serve God when they are comfortable and rich. I have also seen some people serve God when things are very hard for them and as soon as they get up on their feet, they turned away from the affairs of the kingdom of God. In all circumstance, always serve the Lord with all you have.

Saul was a man that disappointed God through an act of unfaithfulness. He did not keep the word of the Lord during his reign as the king of Israel, despite this fact, he consulted with some medium for guidance without referencing the heavenly father for victory. This singular decision resulted to his own death and that of his sons in the hands of the philistines. God turned His back on him because he did not put his trust in Him. In addition, Saul consulted with mere mortal for the battle ahead not realizing that victory can always come by faith in Christ Jesus.

When a man is unfaithful, God will scatter him among men which can make such man unproductive because he will not be in one accord with everyone around him. Unfaithfulness to God breeds famine in the land, makes the land desolate and the end thereof is destruction.

DISOBEDIENCE

A nation or human that is disobedient to God's commandments and laws would not experience the gift of life through Christ our Lord. It is very important as Christians that we obey God's word and laws in order for us to live a purposeful life. There is an underlying spiritual rule according to the heavenly principle for His chosen ones, and it is mandatory for us as Christians to ensure that we observe these rules for us to live a life worthy in the presence of God. When a nation or an individual is disobedient to God's laws and commandments, there are several negative consequences such as penury and consistent plague which could present itself in any form that is detrimental to man's future and the future of the unborn generation.

The greatest of all God's commandments is love. When a human refuses to be at peace and also wishes evil against everyone he or she comes in contact with, he portrays disobedience to the word of God and curse be upon such a man that disobeys God. There are some people that profess to know and serve God with all of their heart, but their lifestyles and deeds deny him in all ramifications. When a man feels very comfortable in sin, there is not doubt that such a soul has been marked for eternal destruction. It is foolishness to indulge in sin and to be disobedient to God's word.

When God created man on earth, He gave specific instructions and commandments to the first man and expected men to abide by these commandments. But through lost and greed, the first man disobeyed God. God commanded Adam and Eve not to eat from the tree, after a period of time in the garden, the devil began to plant in the heart of the woman greed and desire to be like God which obviously cannot happen. The devil knew and understands human nature because he was part of creation, so he capitalized on human weakness which led to disobeying the commandments of God. We the offsprings of the first man are currently suffering the consequences of this act of disobedience.

Pharaoh despite several warnings through the prophet to let the children of Israelite go, he refused and disregarded the commandment of God through a reprobate heart. Despite all the plagues that visited Egypt, he did not hearken to the voice of the Lord. Despite God's warning through his prophet Moses to the king, he refused to obey the word of the Lord.

Jonah the son of Amittai, an Israelite was a man that God had tremendous plan for during his time on earth. Despite several instances when God called him to work with him, he refused to listen to God. He was given a specific instruction by God to prophesy against the wickedness of the city of Nineveh, but he refused. God is not a man that a mere mortal can deceive. Jonah strategically tried to shy away from divine responsibilities assigned to him by God. In an attempt to run away from his assignment, he left on a voyage instead, and on their way, they experienced a stormy weather and soon afterwards, the sailors and crew discovered that Jonah was responsible for the storm they faced in the deep sea. The question is, how did they know Jonah was the reason for the storm, I must tell you that it is by the magnificent power of our Lord. He was thrown into the deep sea and immediately a whale swallowed him and transported him back to where God originally wanted him in order to fulfill the assigned assignment.

CHAPTER SEVEN

WAYS OF TAPPING INTO GOD'S DIVINE PURPOSE

Spiritual Separation from Men

> *Now when these things had been completed, the princes approached me, saying, "The people of Israel and the priests and the Levites have not separated themselves from the peoples of the lands, according to their abominations, those of the Canaanites, the Hittites, the Perizzites, the Jebusites, the Ammonites, the Moabites, the Egyptians and the Amorites. Ezra 9:1 NASB*

A critical look at Abraham and Lot, it was discovered that not until Abraham departed from Lot spiritually, his purpose was not manifested.

Abraham was a man filled with the power of the Holy Ghost and he had a covenant with our creator to establish His kingdom on Earth, but his continuous cohabitation with Lot hindered God's manifestation of his blessings and purpose. Listen very carefully, you must depart from some people in order for your purpose to come into manifestation. There are some people or things in your life that you must let go whether physically or spiritually. When it has to do with individual relationship which could be anyone you are constantly in touch with, such person or group of people has to be eradicated in your life. It could be anything that you keep your friends, colleagues, environment, and so on. Not until a drastic decision is taken, things might not work out as planned.

Discovering who to depart from does not come from a mere mortal observation, but only by the spirit of God who will teach, show, and direct you on who that particular person is that needs to depart from you. In order for you to have a perfect knowledge of this revelation, you need the help of the Holy Trinity to discern in the spiritual realm for a manifestation in the physical.

Spiritual Life

> *Ye have not chosen me, but I have chosen you, and ordained you, that ye should go and bring forth fruit, and that your fruit should remain: that whatsoever ye shall ask of the father in my name, he may give it you. John 15:16 KJV*

You are no more God's servant having recognized who you are and what you are made of in our Lord Jesus Christ. God said that when you keep His commandments, you are no more His servant because if you take a close look at the relationship between a servant and his master, you will notice that there is this kind of formal relationship between both parties. In such a scenario, there is no intimacy between these two parties and the servant knows not what the master is involved in. That is why Jesus Christ said you are no more His servant but His friend by keeping His words and He will reveal what is known to Him by the spirit of God.

He said unto Peter and Andrew, "come and I will make thee fishers of men." Jesus Christ said He has loved us and still loves us and has chosen us in order for us to reproduce and be fruitful in the vineyard of God. How is your spiritual life? Are you battling with sin? He said, "I have ordained you that you should bring forth fruit and your fruit should remain and increase with no price attached to it."

You are of God and cannot be hidden. Your spirit is the candle of the Lord which searches all the unwanted parts of your belly. The very day you were given birth to, He ordained you to be a blessing to the world and to use this blessing as a medium to win more souls for the heavenly kingdom. You have a particular talent which you are expected to apply to that empirical life situation to cause positive changes in lives around you.

Your spiritual life is the most important aspect of your life. You cannot do anything without Christ and by the reason of this fact, you have the ability and power to live above sin; this is because you have the spirit of God inside of you which is the life you have and the light of your life. If you are born again or rather given your life to Christ, you are a new creature; old things have passed away and everything has become new. You cannot struggle with sin because your mortal body has been revitalized and you are not of this world. It is the people of this world that struggle with sin.

I remember when I was still in the university, I took it upon myself that I would at least try to talk to one person about who Christ is every day. With this desire to win souls for Christ, I could present it as a question such as, do you really know that Christ loves you? This will result to more details of how He does love us His creation, and this has really assisted me in affecting lives around me. You could tell this person that Christ loves him or her, and this singular action can change the person's entire life. You do not have any excuse on that day when the trumpet shall sound. God is going to ask you, where were you when you saw that brother going astray? I pray you will not get an answer of "depart from me oh ye worker of iniquity"; I know you not. There are so many people around you moving toward the wide road of destruction and you feel it is not your responsibility to call this person and talk to him or her about Christ. There are so many people who have not heard about the word of God and you have the opportunity to go and visit such deserted area, or even if you cannot go, your substance can still go there but you hardened your heart. Your excuse might be that you are too busy with your business which made it impossible for you to participate, not knowing that you cannot be so busy for the things of the gospel. Do not take the things of this world more importantly than the things of the Lord. Seek ye first the kingdom of God and his righteousness, and all other things shall be added unto you. There are rewards attached to you abiding by the word of God. God is not man that he should lie.

I want you to take this as a responsibility to tell someone everyday that Jesus Christ loves him or her. This can save a soul going astray. I know you are blessed and I know you can positively affect someone close to you with the blessing that God has bestowed upon you.

True Confession

> *That if thou shalt confess with thy mouth the Lord Jesus, and shalt believe in thine heart that God hath raised him from the dead, thou shalt be saved. Romans 10:9 KJV*

> *Labor not for the meat which perisheth, but for that meat which endureth unto everlasting life, which the son of man shall give unto you: for him hath God the father sealed. John 6:27 KJV*

You are not of this world; you are divinely packaged and designed by God for greatness, wonders, and miracles. He wants everlasting life for your soul, and this can only come through when you do not labor in things that are of this world or things that perish but rather you lay up for yourself treasures of the heavens and not of the world.

Many folks in this present generation take the things of God for granted. Such individuals are more concerned with the riches and worldly things more than the things of God, and It has been boldly written in the scriptures that these things perisheth because they are not an everlasting investment but a temporal one. When you ask so many youths of our present-day generation what they would like to become in the nearest future, you will be surprised by their response. We are no more conscious of the things of the spirit but things of the flesh, and as you know the flesh perisheth. The Lord wants more workers in His vineyard, and that is one of the major reasons for your creation. He needs you to work for Him, as this can only take you to everlasting life and God's divine packaged blessings for your life. Your only task as regards your responsibility on this Earthly place is to believe in Him and pass this unto as many people as you can. The only source where you can get eternal life is through the scripture in Christ Jesus; this is because it is the only source of revelation of the things of God lined out for your life.

> *In my father's house there are many mansions: if it were not so, I would have told you. I go to prepare a place for you. And if I go and prepare a place for you, I will come again, and receive you unto myself; that where I am, there ye may be also. John 14:2–3 KJV*

Christ said He has gone to prepare a place for you; isn't it nice for you to at least see where has been prepared for you as He waits for your arrival? It would be quite unfortunate if you will not be a partaker of the divine and sacrificial offering by Christ. You need to inherit the kingdom of God because it is your inheritance and you are entitled to it; it is your right, but there are adversaries who will not stop until you miss this inheritance. These adversaries are always there to steal and kill your birthright. But I have good news for you: Jesus is the way, the truth, and the life; no man cometh unto the father but through Him. He is the only mediator to reaching God. If you believe in Christ, you believe in God. I am very sure and convinced you would not want to miss this everlasting life God has destined for you to inherit.

Being Born Again

According to John 3 (NIV), Jesus answered, "I tell you the truth, no one can enter the kingdom of God unless he is born of water and the Spirit. Flesh gives birth to flesh, but the Spirit gives birth to spirit. You should not be surprised at my saying, You must be born again. Being born again means you are absolutely surrendering unto God your whole life. When you are born again, you are not the old person you used to be; behold you are now a new creature who has come to achieve one of your most important purposes. When you are born again, it means you have come to the realization of God's divine purpose for your life. Being born again gives you joy, peace, and blessing from God. You are no more of this world. You have now become a supernatural being on Earth because you are now operating under the influence of the spirit of God who will teach you everything.

The most exciting experience in life is being a born-again Christian; this is because when you are born again, you henceforth cease to battle with life circumstances on your own. God will fight your battles. But it surprises me when I hear people say that living a life of Christ is the most difficult thing to do on Earth. Ignorantly, this idea is from the bottomless pit of hell that has lead men astray, and it is packaged to lead men to the part of destruction. Living a godly life is the easiest life to practice on Earth. When you are born again, you live above sin, you do not struggle with sin. You will always get inspiration and vision by the help of the Holy Spirit, and you will be filled with anointing of the Holy Spirit of God. No weapon formed nor fashioned against you shall prosper; the heavenly host would fight on your behalf. Do you know what it means for the heavenly host to fight on your behalf? The Bible says you will possess the Earth, and there would not be any room for sickness or diseases in your body nor around you, because your presence carries anointing that breaks the yoke. You are now an offspring born of God and henceforth you are now the property of God.

When you are born again, you inherit the kingdom of God (John 3:3). You cannot do without Christ in your life in this world, for He is your helper in this world. You are not of this world but of heaven, and that is your everlasting home that has been prepared for you. I pray that you will receive the power to realize this important decision in your life.

Believe in God

> *Some trust in chariots and some in horses, but we trust in the name of the Lord our God.*
>
> *They are brought to their knees and fall, but we rise up and stand firm. Psalm 20:7-8 NIV*

Believing in Christ means putting your entire trust in Him. Take, for example, a situation where a man entrusts his survival on a particular Element, this means that all hope is placed on this element for the continuous and future existence of this man. When you put your trust in God, it is one way you can gain access to the things of the heavenly throne. It is the first criterion to work with God. It brings you closer to an everlasting life that has been prepared for you. He is the bread of life; anyone who eats from Him shall not thirst anymore. He is the only one that can give you everlasting water that would not make you thirst anymore. When you believe in Christ, He would help you, and He would provide for your needs and uplift you. Not only that, He would increase you in all spheres of life. When you put your trust in Him, you will not be condemned to everlasting torture. You need to trust and put your faith in Him for all your desires which can only come based on the fundamental knowledge you have in His word. He is always there to supply all your needs. All you need to do is go to Him in prayers, supplication, and thanksgiving, and then watch the surprise that would come your way because you now operate under His love and direction. He loves you and that is why He came purposely to redeem you from all unfortunate life circumstances by His death on the cross of Calvary. Put your trust in Him and He would not fail you.

When you believe in God, He would always put answers to your prayers. When you believe in God, He will constantly make a way for you when there seems to be no way because He knows all hope is placed on Him for a meaningful life on earth. God knows what you need and He will make it a primary responsibility to provide for your needs. Isn't that wonderful? So why not put your trust and believe in Him for that particular thing you are hoping for? We as Christians will continually put our trust in the Lord our God, but some people may put their trust in whatsoever they believe can save them which obviously will not give them a happy end because they will be brought to their knees and fall but we will always stand tall and strong because we believe in God.

Keeping God's Commandment

Christ has come that you might have life and have it more abundantly. He gave us commandments, and among these commandments, the greatest of all is "love." He said, "Thou shall love the Lord thy God and obey His commandments and thou shall love thy neighbor as you love yourself." You need to keep these commandments; by this singular decision, you can inherit the kingdom of God. Christ gave Christians the opportunity to live a life of the celestial world by His teachings, and in the process of His teachings, He told us of the greatest of all His commandments which is love. This is the only instruction of Christ to us the chosen ones because we are not of this world. You owe Him and you have a 100% obligation to obey His commandments; it is the yardstick for eternal judgment. You need to love one another and serve God with all your heart, obey His words, and pray for one another. When you start living a life of love, you will notice a great change in your life. When you obey His commandments, your spirit will be lightened which will enable you ascend to the celestial world when you depart from this temporal place of human existence. The celestial world is a place of spiritual maturity for human souls to ascend to the iluminous height. When you practice love, it brings you to eternal glory and salvation. Salvation can only come when you obey His commandments (John 13:34).

In Him was life and this life has been passed unto us which makes us the light of the world, and the life of Christ is the light which is in us, the chosen generation. Christ has come to give us an unmerited grace, and He also brought truth for the redemption of man in this world. When you keep His commandment, you are above condemnation and every failure of life. Keeping His commandments enables you to operate under His grace and protection which helps you carry on with life's circumstances. Christ has come so that you might have life and have it more abundantly. You need to start operating under the influence and umbrella of the Almighty for therein are the blessings and salvation of the chosen ones. He has a surprise package for you which is awaiting your arrival, and this surprise gift is unmerited by you. He loves you and that is why He constantly ensures that all your needs are taken care of.

Beloved you are born to be fruitful in every area of your life. But one very important criterion for this privilege to be available to you is keeping His commandments. He has spoken into your life to be fruitful, and this you shall pass unto your unborn generation by working with Him faithfully. He has started something good in your life, something great that would exceed your expectation.

I can tell you that every disappointment in the past concerning your life will turn out to be a supernatural appointment, and all the disgrace over your life will turn out to be God's grace in all you do. Every failure in your life will turn out to be a success in every aspect of your life in Jesus' name. God wants the best for you, and this is the more reason why He gave you power over everything on Earth. He has said and pronounced in your life to be fruitful. God's word cannot go void but until it accomplishes what it is assigned to accomplish. God is not a man that he should lie; our God is not a God that lies and He cannot lie because He is God of the heavens and Earth, He created the heavens, Earth, and all that is within it. Fruitfulness comes with a proper reflection of your life and your relationship with the trinity and sincerely reconciling your old ways that is unpleasing to God.

> *The earth is the Lord's and the fullness thereof; the world and they that dwell therein. Psalm 24:1 KJV*

Obviously, from the above scripture, it is observed that the world is of the Lord and everything that is in it and God has given us the power and ability to rule over the Earth. My advice is for you is to sit down in your closet and reflect back into your past life and understand where you have gone wrong and also simultaneously reconcile your ways with God. This aspect of your life is one of the most important things that you cannot deny in order to come to the realization of who you really are. You need to reflect back into your life and what you have done in the past for restitution. Is it pleasing in the sight of God? This is necessary because it will go a long way to affect your future and how easily you can come to the understanding and operation of the word of God concerning your life. Reflecting back into your past life will help you learn from your past which will help in correcting your mistakes and prevent this from occurring in the nearest future. Are you the type of person that feels not worthy to stand before the Lord? He said that you should come unto His throne with a heart of reconciliation and thanksgiving for He is ready to take you in and forgive all your sins. He is a God that is always ready to forgive your sins if you are sincere with yourself. Do you know that you have the power to live above sin? You have to get this clear, you can and have the ability inside of you to live above sin as your old man (your past life) was crucified with Him on the cross and the body of sin has been destroyed in you, and henceforth you should and can never serve sin because you bear the mark of Christ on you.

> *Knowing this, that our old man is crucified with him, that the body of sin might be destroyed, that henceforth we should not serve sin. Romans 6:6 KJV*

Understanding the fact about who you are and what you are made up of enables you to withstand the storm in an ocean of confusion, deception, sin, penury, and a life that is full of debts. His grace is sufficient for you to always do what is right in His sight and to also live a virtuous life. Do you know that you cannot live a life full of sin? You were dead to sin on the cross and buried with Him by the baptism of the Holy Ghost into death, for death and sin cannot have dominion over you.

You need a proper reflection of your life to discover the covered revelation and secret places that have covered your blessing. If you are still not satisfied with your present state, it simply means that there are some things that have not been revealed which have really served as a hindrance to the effectiveness of your God-given potentials in your life. In order to amaze people around you, you need to have someone greater than anything you can think of in this world that would teach and direct you to the path of great exploit, and that is Jesus Christ. Our God is the God of yesterday, today, and forever; He knows your past, and the only way you can have foresight of the future is to genuinely repent. He is always ready to forgive you and to also reconcile all your transgressions; He is always ready to blot them out. All you need to do is observe a proper reflection of your life and do not allow the past things nor consider the things of the old to decide your future because it might serve as hindrance to your purpose.

> *There is therefore now no condemnation to them which are in Christ Jesus, who walk not after the flesh, but after the spirit. Romans 8:1 KJV*

One very interesting word according to the scripture above is the word "now" which simply means present tense. He is not bothered about your past but is concerned about your present and future. That is why He said, "There is therefore 'now' no condemnation upon your life for Christ has not condemned you"; no man on Earth has the power and ability to condemn your life. You are in Christ Jesus by working according to His principles of life and also working after the spirit of God. You are greater than any form of condemnation in your life. The Bible says, "Cast your burden on Him and He will sustain you and will not suffer you."

The promise of God has not changed in your life and can never change. He is a God that keeps to promise; He is not a promise breaker; He is the God that said that over two million years ago and will still say today because He is a God that change not:

> *Jesus Christ the same yesterday and today and forever. Hebrews 13:8 KJV*

He is a God of the past, the present, and the future. He works in miraculous ways and He has a great plan for your life. Your friend cannot always be there for you, but He is always there no matter the circumstances you are currently going through.

You were not just created for creation's sake. Do you know that there is something so special about you that is yet to be revealed to your understanding and this is as a result of your inability to put God's word to active use in your life? Do you know you are fearfully and wonderfully made by God? When God was creating you, it took Him time through some careful process because you were created uniquely and you are different from other humans around on Earth. The sooner you come to the realization of this fact that you are specially and wonderfully made, the better for you.

If you do not mind, go to the mirror and take a good look at yourself with a smile; you will notice this unique and wonderful nature of Christ in you. You were created in His own image after His own likeness. Do you know you are more than what people think you are? Because you bear the mark of Christ in you.

> *Ye are of God, little children and have overcome them: because greater is he that is in you, than he that is in the world. 1 John 4:4 KJV*

Get this straight, you are created for a particular purpose on Earth, and the sooner you realize this fact, the better. The realization of this fact will guide and direct you in all you do. You have something inside of you that needs to be activated. God has a genuine reason for your creation. You weren't created just to fill in an empty space on Earth. For example, take the life of our Lord Jesus Christ on Earth; He came into this world primarily for the redemption and salvation of mankind, as well as for reconciling God and man together. Christ's major purpose on Earth was to come and die for you, for the salvation of your soul and to also liberate you and me from our old life and bring us into the presence of His father for the salvation of our soul.

Taking a good look at the life of Jesus Christ on Earth, you will discover that He accomplished His purpose on Earth by the help of the Holy Ghost and was crucified by the help of the devil ignorantly not knowing he was set for eternal damnation through that channel of Jesus Christ's crucifixion. Ignorantly, the anti-Christ was doing the right thing, but when he came to the realization of his mistake, Christ had already taken His glory on Earth and in heaven. A close look at your life, you will discover that you bear the mark of Christ in you; this means you can do all things through Christ that strengthens you, and all you need is the Holy Spirit and anointing which breaks the yoke. You have been given the power to overcome the world through Christ Jesus.

Do you know that you will be held accountable for how you lived your life on Earth? For Christ has made it clear that you were created for a particular reason and this reason must be achieved while you are on Earth. Kindly note that if this reason is not achieved while you operate on the face of the Earth, who will then fulfill your own purpose on Earth when you have gone to the world beyond? This means that you have failed in all other ramifications of life. When you die, your flesh which permitted your spirit man to live on this Earth is no longer important; this is because your real being (your spirit) is no longer making effective use of that envelope (your flesh), for the dead has no business on the surface of the Earth, because after death comes judgment. On that day, you and I will account for all activities of our lives and how we lived during our transition on planet Earth. So, you have all the opportunity now to re-strategize your plan of knowing and achieving your God-given purpose on Earth.

A positive impact on people's lives is very important in our race for eternity. Creating an impact is a channel or mechanism of affecting lives around you. This impact can be positive and can also be negative. Positive impartation is the goal of any Christian who aspires the kingdom of God and who has the spirit of God in his or her life. You impact positively the lives of those around you by the impact you have made on their physical, spiritual, psychological, and mental wellbeing and making sure that these people are always happy. We are God's chosen people.

You can also positively impact the lives of those around you by your words of encouragement. Life and death are in the power of your tongue; it contains prosperity and destruction depending on how you put into active use the words that proceedeth out of your heart. Learn to speak words of blessing, healing, prosperity, and peace in the lives of those around you. Out of your mouth comes the issues of life and death. Always learn to speak words that can give hope to the hopeless and life to the lifeless; you can transform lives by what you say, and only if you choose to transform life in a way that will be pleasing in the sight of God that you will be operating in the direction of God's plan for a particular life. Do you know that you will be held responsible for those lives you apparently saw going astray and you never bothered to say anything to transform such lives?

> *This is my commandment, that ye love one another, as I have loved you. John 15:12 KJV*

I also want to reiterate that our Lord Jesus Christ has come not to condemn the old commandments but to bring humanity and human creation into the new commandments that conceptualize the Ten Commandments into one which is love. Love is the greatest of all; it brings joy, happiness, and blessings of God into the lives of His chosen ones. It helps to achieve your purpose in life because it brings you closer to God which helps you for direction, natural instinct, and intuition which brings you into focus and realization of His plan for your life.

Do you know that whatever you do to the least of your brothers and sisters around you, you do unto God? I will not relent in emphasizing the importance of making this world a better place through your good deed(s). Whenever you see those hungry around you, those that have no food to eat, how do you feel and react to their situation? If you watch closely, they are dying of hunger, and if you refuse to help, God is watching. There are so many people who need your help financially, materially, spiritually, and so on. There are so many sick people around you, and they need your love and words of healing for their lives and you refuse to hearken to the voice of God to help. There are so many people who need the word of God in prisons, and some are condemned to death while you are rejoicing in the little world of your own. You can help these sets of people in any possible way you can through the gospel. God has given you the ability and strength to help. If you cannot go, who will then voluntarily go to help these people from the precarious situation they are facing?

> *Be not deceived, God is not mocked; for whatsoever a man soweth, that shall he also reap. Galatians 6:7 KJV*

Get this folks, it is what you sow that you will reap. The amount of effort or input that you put into any work or activity determines the result or output of such an activity. Your input and impact in life and on those around you determines what you get in return when your physical body departs unto eternity. A farmer who plants yam cannot expect to reap beans; the more you sow, the more you reap. The moment you lack the necessary ingredient of how the basic principle(s) of sowing and reaping operates, that marks the beginning of an unpleasant harvest. This also applies to our lives as Christians. You cannot expect to reap the same benefit as those that sow more than you, for if you sow ten dollars, you are expected to reap the benefit of ten dollars.

You need to show love to those around you, make them feel important, care for them, give them hope, and help those who need your help. They don't have to necessarily come to you; it can be ministered unto you to do something for them, and I tell you, the moment you receive that word, do not hesitate as it might serve as a means for God to test your love for Him (keeping His commandment). God loves a cheerful giver and it is more blessed to give than to receive. As you give, you are sowing into your life abundant blessings in all spheres of life which brings into your life prosperity that is continuous (Deuteronomy 15:7–11).

Having answered the above questions, the major concern of this book is made manifest by the power of the Holy Spirit which is your divine purpose on Earth by God. As I have always said, every man on Earth has a purpose, and not until you come to this realization, you will be operating in a realm that is below your divine and ordained position. The sooner you realize your purpose, the better you become a blessing to generations yet unborn.

Do you remember the parable of our Lord Jesus Christ, Lazarus and the rich man? It was recorded that while on earth, the rich man had everything in his possession but Lazarus did not. Lazarus continually ate remnants on the ground while the rich man ignored his presence. The rich man deliberately ignored Lazarus for some inexplicable reasons best known to him. One day, they both died and met on the other side of the heavenly creation, and it was recorded in the Bible that the rich man was tormented in hell and Lazarus was with the angels, the saints and the heavenly creations witnessing God's covenant with the chosen generation. You still have the opportunity to turn around; there are so many Lazarus' around you who needs your help, you can still show love and blessings to their lives in a way that would benefit you and the rest of the world. Christ said, "If you love me, keep my commandment which is the greatest of all, "love" (John 14:15).

Some people were born into a home of wealth and some people were born into a household that automatically places them in an inequality equation through abject poverty. Does this now mean that those that were privileged to be born into wealth should use this as an opportunity to oppress the poor? If you fall into the first category, I urge you to please use this wealth as a blessing to the less privileged among and not as a curse. According to studies, life expectancy is on the downward trend. So many people die at their early age due to several precarious factors. When your soul departs your flesh, what will be explanation to our heavenly father when you face the judgement throne? I am not saying that all rich men and women will not inherit the kingdom of God, but it is the lack of spiritual sensitivity of some rich among us towards the poor that will inevitably lead them towards the path of eternal destruction. The riches God has placed on your care is specifically programmed for a purpose. You should be heavenly conscious with a heart of love.

You need to start seeing yourself as a different person in all ramifications of life. God has said it, "If you love me, keep my commandment." All you need to do now is to exercise the word of God in your life. I don't know your present situation; all I know is that you have not come across this book by chance but by the grace of God for your life because I know that you have already started operating in the realm of your divine purpose by virtue of coming across the word of God.

You are a royal priesthood, a city set on a hill that cannot be hidden; you are born to be fruitful in all areas of your life. Have you seen a situation where the son of a king lacks? To the best of my knowledge, it is impossible because God has lifted you up in the highest place and has not made the world to rejoice over you. You are a prince and princess of this world and Christ is the king of this world, which gives you the opportunity to have everything at your disposal. Start operating as a king and queen on Earth because everything on Earth belongs to you. Start to exercise your authority now!

In conclusion, as a Christian, your commitment, knowledge and hardwork will help bring good result and catapult you to a great height. Your attitude will take you to a greater height but the love of God will always take you to the greatest height. It is also important to note that Christians need to know and understand that the love of God supersedes all infirmities and circumstances they are passing through. There are countless number of persecutions and hatred towards the chosen generation, but I encourage you to count it all joy because your reward is in heaven. Keep up the good and hardwork as we wait for the coming of our heavenly father in glory through Jesus Christ. God bless you.

CPSIA information can be obtained
at www.ICGtesting.com
Printed in the USA
LVHW031642210121
677113LV00004B/718

9 781489 730480